FINCH BAKERY

FINCH BAKERY

SWEET HOMEMADE TREATS & SHOWSTOPPER CELEBRATION CAKES

LAUREN & RACHEL FINCH

CONTENTS

WELCOME TO FINCH BAKERY

We first started the bakery from our parent's kitchen just before our 21st birthday, making a three-tiered, wobbly, wonky mess of a cake that reignited our childhood love for baking. Over the years as our skills grew, baking for family and friends became more than a hobby and we opened our first shop on Queen Street in Great Harwood, Lancashire in 2016.

From there, Finch Bakery has grown from a small front counter offering a few dozen treats each day to selling hundreds of cookies, brownies, cupcakes, rocky roads and – everybody's favourite – cake jars, both instore and online. Now, with an incredible 30-strong team working over three sites and creating all kinds of delectable treats, we've just opened a new flagship store on Queen Street.

Our customers travel from all over and queue down the street of our small Lancastrian town to get their fix of Finch goodies, but while being closed for over a year through the global pandemic, we shifted our focus to online delivery so that no-one would have to go without their favourite brownies, cookies and cake jars. We also started selling our own range of equipment and partnered with our favourite baking brands so that you can all create your own Finch treats at home.

We started Finch Bakery with no expectations. From our simple love for baking cakes and with the support of family, friends, our amazing team, and, of course, our incredible legion of fans and customers, both online and local, the business has grown beyond our wildest dreams. We are so proud to be able to inspire others to start baking – whether for your own business or just for pleasure, we hope that by sharing some of our most sought-after tips, tricks and techniques, we can help you to create your own wonderful bakes at home.

Many of our recipes are really versatile, so we encourage you to experiment with flavours and decorating techniques to suit your own style and taste – you might not always get it perfect the first time (we don't either!) but we hope you have fun as your baking skills and confidence grow. Whether you are one of our long-time followers or just starting out with baking – we hope it's one delicious journey!

FINCH BASICS

EQUIPMENT

From essential tools that you may already have at home to specialist baking equipment that can help to give your cakes a professional finish, here is the equipment we couldn't do without.

MIXER / HAND-HELD ELECTRIC WHISK

Most recipes in this book call for a mixer. We use a KitchenAid, however, there are so many other brilliant mixers available to choose from as well. If you don't have a mixer, you can use a hand-held electric whisk instead.

CAKE & BAKING TINS

Each recipe in this book uses either a 20cm (8in) round or a 20 x 30cm (8 x 12in) rectangular tin. If you want to replace a rectangular tin with a square one, use a 23cm (9in) tin. We recommend rectangular and square tins that have straight sides (rather than tapered sides) to ensure even bakes. We use Silverwood cake tins.

SILICONE MOULDS

The newest craze in the cake world, you can buy silicone moulds in practically every shape and size. These are great for creating filled chocolate shells and tempered chocolate shapes.

CAKE DRUMS

We prefer to use cake drums, which are slightly thicker than cake boards, to create a stable base for all of our celebration cakes. A cake drum should be at least 7.5cm (3in) wider than the un-iced cake to accommodate the crumb coat, buttercream layer and a decorative border around the base of the cake, if required.

WEIGHING SCALES

Combining baking ingredients can be an exact science, which is why recipes call for accurate measurements – it's best to use electric scales.

ANGLED PALETTE KNIFE

You can use this versatile tool to apply, smooth and make patterns in buttercream, lift cookies and macarons from baking trays, spread batter, or apply gel food colouring, among many things.

CAKE SCRAPERS

We use our own range of metal cake scrapers, but there are plenty of metal, acrylic and plastic versions available. Essential for achieving a smooth finish or adding patterns such as stripes or a zig-zag to buttercream, a cake scraper is a must-have for impressive cake decoration.

PIPING BAGS AND NOZZLES

Good-quality piping bags are vital for successful piping – we recommend large, anti-slip eco or biodegradable plastic piping bags. Owning every single nozzle is not imperative; start off with a couple of open and closed star nozzles and build your collection as your skills grow.

MACARON MAT

Use a macaron mat to ensure perfectly even macarons every time. They are available online, or alternatively, you can print a paper template to use underneath high quality baking parchment. There are also different shaped macaron templates available to trace such as hearts, bears, unicorns and many others.

PASTRY BRUSH

We use a pastry brush (or sometimes a paint brush) to wash the sugar off the sides of a pan to prevent it from burning, to create chocolate brush strokes, to apply cake release to tins and to apply gold or silver leaf to the side of cakes.

SUGAR THERMOMETER

A couple of recipes in this book call for a sugar thermometer to ensure the correct temperature is met. This is for several different reasons including killing bacteria, tempering chocolate and ensuring sugar will take on its correct form.

SPIRIT LEVEL

Yes, you read that correctly; we used to use a (clean!) spirit level after trimming the top of a sponge to ensure all of the layers were level. These days we have invested in an expensive cake leveller called Agbay, which saves time and ensures perfectly level cakes every time.

TURNTABLE

A good turntable ensures buttercream goes on evenly and prevents constantly having to move the cake. We recommend a heavy-duty metal one rather than plastic, to ensure the weight of the cake is supported and the turntable rotates smoothly to make decorating so much easier.

DOWELS

Cake dowels are wooden or plastic straws or sticks. They are pushed into a cake to add stability to it, and are essential for tiered cakes to make sure the layers don't move or collapse.

INGREDIENTS

Most ingredients in this book can be bought from supermarkets, excluding some specialist items such as bake-stable chocolate chips, certain types of spreads, chocolate and specialist flavourings. Here are a few things to note regarding the ingredients we use.

EGGS

All of our recipes use UK medium (US large) free-range eggs.

BUTTER

Unless specified otherwise, butter should be softened and at room temperature before using.

FOOD COLOURING

There are many brands out there, but we mainly use Wilton, Sugarflair and Colour Mill.

WHITENERS

There are lots of icing and buttercream whiteners on the market, including white colouring gels and whitening powders. We use whitening powder to create a super white buttercream. If you do not have any whitener, we recommend whipping the butter for 5–10 minutes before adding the icing sugar. You can also add a pin prick amount of purple food colouring to counteract the yellow.

DECORATIONS

Most quality decorations such as sprinkles, lustre dusts, gold and silver leaf, and gel or oil food colouring are available to purchase from specialist baking shops or online.

LINING TINS

Whether you are baking brownies, cookies or celebration cakes, lining tins with baking parchment is an essential step when preparing your baked goods. Whilst you may have always greased your tins with butter alone, using baking parchment achieves high-quality bakes with even sides. As it is anti-stick, it also prevents any tearing when removing the cake from the tin, as well as over-browning.

HOME-MADE CAKE RELEASE

Makes 330g (11½oz) or about 1 jam jar
110g (½ cup) vegetable shortening
110g (½ cup) vegetable oil
110g (1 scant cup) plain flour

If you've ever struggled getting your cakes out of obscure shaped tins (think spheres, skulls and bundt tins!), and greasing with butter just doesn't work, this is the quick and simple recipe for you. Cakes and cookie cups will slide right out of the tins after using this method:

Soften the vegetable shortening and whip in a mixer until creamed. Add the oil and mix again.

Sift in the flour and whip on high until it is very smooth and white in colour.

To use, paint generously into cake and cupcake tins with a pastry brush before adding batter and baking as usual. Store in an airtight container in the fridge for up to a year. Soften in the microwave at full power before using.

LINING A BAKING TRAY

Baking trays covered in baking parchment are perfect for baking cookies of all shapes and sizes. The parchment helps reduce hot and cool spots within the oven, reduces spreading and, of course, prevents anything sticking to the tray, creating an evenly baked cookie.

It's as simple as drawing around your baking tray directly onto the baking parchment, cutting it out and securing down with a little butter or oil onto the tray.

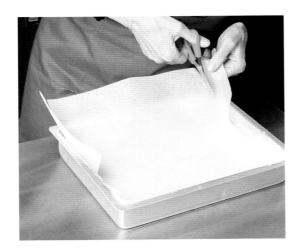

LINING A SQUARE BAKING TIN

Lay out the baking parchment and place the square or rectangular tin on top with space all around. Draw around the base of the tin with a pencil. Measure the depth of the tin and add it on around the whole square or rectangle.

Cut a strip of parchment slightly longer than the length of the long side of the tin. Grease the entire tin with butter or oil and stick the strip to the tin overlapping the corners.

From both edges on the long side of the larger piece of parchment, make two vertical cuts where the original base is drawn onto the baking parchment.

Slide the uncut edge up to the strip, then gently ease the parchment into the tin and up the sides. When the base is in place, ease the cut flaps inwards and stick down with a little more butter or oil.

Fill the tin with your desired batter and bake in the oven.

When removing the parchment, wait until the bake has cooled completely.

LINING A ROUND BAKING TIN

If you are lining one tin, place the base of the tin directly onto the baking parchment and draw around the edge with a pencil. Cut the circle out neatly with a pair of scissors. If you are lining multiples of the same tin, fold the parchment over as many times as tins you have and then draw around the base. Cut the layered parchment neatly following the guide of the circle to achieve several perfectly cut circles.

Cut long strips of baking parchment, a little thicker than the depth of the tin, and fold the parchment 2.5cm (1in) up from the bottom. Use the scissors to snip upwards towards the fold leaving around 2.5cm (1in) in-between each snip.

Grease the tin using either butter or oil and stick the long strip around the sides of the tin, angling it down. Make sure the squares you have snipped lay flat around the bottom of the tin.

Place the circle of parchment into the bottom of the tin over the top of the flat squares.

Fill the tin with your desired batter and bake in the oven.

When removing the parchment, wait until the bake has cooled completely.

COLOURINGS

There are a variety of different products on the market, and each one can affect the taste or texture of whatever you are colouring.

LIQUID

Water-based liquid food colouring is often the first thing home bakers reach for on the supermarket shelves due to its accessibility and cost. However, the colour will be less intense than other options available. The consistency of your bake can also be compromised due to the water content – for this reason we would not use it for macarons. Liquid food colouring is not suitable for colouring chocolate, as the water will split the chocolate and cause it to seize. *Our favourite for: Hard Candy Lollipops (see page 189).*

OIL-BASED

Oil-based food colouring has been developed specifically with chocolate in mind. It contains soya lecithin, which acts as an emulsifier between water and chocolate so that it maintains its fluidity. Oil-based colourings can be used for buttercream and sponges, but are not suitable for macarons. *Our favourite for: Drips (see pages 50–51); Chocolate Shards & Sails (see page 32); White Chocolate Ganache (see page 19); Cakesicles (see page 205). Recommended brands: Colour Mill; Wilton.*

POWDER

Powdered colours are mostly available online and they are great for recipes that call for no extra water. Add a little bit to alcohol or lemon juice to use as an edible paint, or add a small amount at a time to a wet mixture and stir in until fully incorporated. *Our favourite for: Macarons (see page 216); painting chocolate drips.*

PASTE

The colour in these is highly pigmented so a little goes a long way – a tiny dab on the end of a cocktail stick is enough! It is best to build up the shade bit by bit. Sometimes streaks of paste can catch and cause inconsistencies in the colour. Nonetheless, it is worth making the investment in some high-quality colourings that will keep in your baking cupboard for ages! *Our favourite for: Buttercream (see pages 16–17); fondant. Recommended brand: Sugarflair.*

GEL

Colouring gels are probably the most versatile product on the market. Gel is similar to paste – slightly less concentrated in colour but still gives really vibrant shades whilst keeping the consistency of your baking mix. Some brands are available in supermarkets, however, we have found these are not as pigmented as those you can buy online. *Our favourite for: Buttercream (see pages 16–17); Macarons (see pages 216–217); sponges; fondant. Recommended brands: Wilton; Magic Colours; Pro Gel.*

NATURAL

Food colourings from natural sources are ideal if you would like to use less synthetic products or if you are baking for people with particular nutritional requirements. Generally, the colourants are derived from plants, such as beetroot, peppers or turmeric, and you only require a small amount of product. They may affect taste if used straight from the natural source and if using a liquid natural food colouring, the colours may not be as vibrant as when using synthetic colours. *Recommended brands/products: PME natural food colouring; beetroot; paprika; turmeric.*

FLAVOURINGS

Extracts and essences are both used to flavour foods, but differ greatly. They are a brilliant way of achieving flavours that would be unobtainable naturally – think candy floss and bubblegum!

VANILLA EXTRACT & ESSENCE

Vanilla extract – generally preferred in baking due to taste and quality – is made from real vanilla beans and is therefore more expensive than essence, which contains synthetic vanilla flavouring. Imitation vanilla is best avoided due to its synthetic taste.

HIGH-STRENGTH FLAVOURINGS

Liquid flavours are amazing for offering variety throughout your bakes. Even natural flavours such as orange and lemon juice are available in oil form; real lemon juice is quite sharp, while oils tend to be sweeter. Flavours such as lemon, orange, peppermint and almond are readily available in most supermarkets and are brilliant for flavouring buttercream.

A high-strength flavouring is particularly useful if you are making a larger batch of sponges or something that cannot tolerate extra water in the recipe, such as macarons. There are different concentrations of flavourings available on the market, with supermarket brands tending to be weaker and needing more product for an intense flavour. *Recommended brand: Foodie Flavours.*

SPRINKLES

Sprinkles have come a long way since the "hundreds and thousands" days. Now available in every colour and shape, sprinkles are our favourite decoration and we use any excuse to throw them on (and in!) our bakes.

BAKE-STABLE SPRINKLES

As sprinkles are just small pieces of sugar, they can easily melt, so sprinkles that are bake-stable are imperative when exposing them to high temperatures, such as our Funfetti Layer Cake (see page 67). These are available on specialist websites. *Recommended brands: Shire Bakery; Super Streusel.*

GOLD & SILVER LEAF / EDIBLE GLITTER

Steer clear of metallic leaf and glitter that is deemed "non toxic", but not edible – these products should not be consumed and are for decoration purposes only. Genuine gold and silver leaf is expensive! Carefully apply loose gold or silver leaf with a dry paintbrush to your bakes. Try not to use your fingers as it will stick to you and most of the product will be lost. Spray edible glitter at a distance from your cake and watch your masterpiece sparkle! There are a range of colours and styles to choose from.
Recommended brand: Barnabas Blattgold.

BUTTERCREAM

One of the most important parts of cake decoration is getting the correct consistency for buttercream. If it is too wet, it won't hold its shape and can melt off the cake; if it's too stiff, you may find it difficult to squeeze through the piping bag. The trick is to soften the butter enough at the start to end up with a silky mixture. It is best made right before you are going to use it, but if you make it in advance and store it in the fridge, you can loosen it up with a splash of warm water or milk and bring it up to room temperature before using. For best results, mix buttercream using a mixer or hand-held electric whisk.

PLAIN BUTTERCREAM

250g (2 sticks) unsalted butter, softened
500g (3½ cups) icing sugar, plus extra if needed

Add the butter to the bowl of a mixer and whip on a high speed for 5 minutes – this may take a little longer if using a hand-held electric whisk. Scrape down the sides of the bowl with a spatula and whip for another 30 seconds. This will turn the butter more white than yellow.

Sift the icing sugar into the bowl and combine on a medium setting, remembering to stop and scrape around the sides to mix in everything fully.

FLAVOURED BUTTERCREAM

250g (2 sticks) unsalted butter, softened
500g (3½ cups) icing sugar, plus extra if needed
Extract of your choice, to taste (almond, peppermint, caramel, candy floss... the list is endless!)

Follow the **PLAIN BUTTERCREAM** method (see above), adding your extract or flavouring of choice. The strength, brand and type of flavouring will determine how much you need – when it comes to extracts, add a little at a time until you reach the required strength of flavour.

VANILLA BUTTERCREAM

250g (2 sticks) unsalted butter, softened
500g (3½ cups) icing sugar, plus extra if needed
1 tsp vanilla extract or vanilla bean paste

Follow the **PLAIN BUTTERCREAM** method (see left). Add the vanilla extract or paste and mix for a further 15 seconds. You can add more extract or paste if you want more flavour.

CHOCOLATE BUTTERCREAM

250g (2 sticks) unsalted butter, softened
500g (3½ cups) icing sugar, plus extra if needed
100g (1 cup) cocoa powder

Follow the **PLAIN BUTTERCREAM** method (see left), but sift in the cocoa powder with the icing sugar. For a darker colour, replace some of the icing sugar with extra cocoa powder.

LEMON BUTTERCREAM

250g (2 sticks) unsalted butter, softened
500g (3½ cups) icing sugar, plus extra if needed
2 tbsp lemon juice or 2 tsp lemon oil
Grated zest of ½ lemon (optional)

Follow the **PLAIN BUTTERCREAM** method (see left). Mix in the lemon juice or oil, 1 teaspoon at a time, and the zest.

CREAM CHEESE BUTTERCREAM

250g (2 sticks) unsalted butter, softened

600g (5 cups) icing sugar, plus extra if needed

180g (6oz) full-fat cream cheese

A dash of lemon juice (optional)

Follow the **PLAIN BUTTERCREAM** method (see page 16). Beat in the cream cheese and lemon juice, if using.

WHIPPED CREAM BUTTERCREAM

250g (9oz) white chocolate

250g (2 sticks) unsalted butter, softened

500g (3½ cups) icing sugar

100ml (6½ tbsp) double cream

Pinch of salt

Gently melt the chocolate and set it aside until it is cool but still liquid. Follow the **PLAIN BUTTERCREAM** method (see page 16), then add the cooled melted chocolate, double cream and salt, and whip for a further 5 minutes.

CHOCOLATE WHIPPED CREAM BUTTERCREAM

250g (9oz) milk chocolate

250g (2 sticks) unsalted butter, softened

450g (3¼ cups) icing sugar

50g (½ cup) cocoa powder

100ml (6½ tbsp) double cream

Pinch of salt

Gently melt the chocolate and set aside until it is cool but still liquid. Follow the **PLAIN BUTTERCREAM** method (see page 16), but sift in the cocoa with the icing sugar. Then, add the cooled melted chocolate, double cream and salt, and whip for a further 5 minutes.

SWISS MERINGUE BUTTERCREAM

240g (1 cup) egg whites or 6 egg whites

400g (2 cups) granulated sugar

400g (3 sticks plus 3 tbsp) unsalted butter, softened and cut into cubes

Vanilla extract or a flavouring of your choice, to taste

Pinch of salt

Gel food colouring (optional)

Special equipment: Sugar thermometer

Whisk together the egg whites and sugar in a heatproof bowl using a hand-held electric whisk, and then place the bowl over a pan of simmering water.

Continue to whisk the egg and sugar mixture until the sugar has dissolved over the heat. Use a sugar thermometer to test the temperature of the egg mixture; it should reach 71°C (160°F) and should not be grainy.

Transfer the mixing bowl to a mixer and beat on a medium speed until the mixture cools. This should take 10–15 minutes. Alternatively, continue mixing with a hand-held electric whisk.

Add the unsalted butter, one cube at a time, continuously whipping until all of the butter has been incorporated. Mix in the vanilla extract or flavouring, salt and any colouring, if using.

TOP TIPS

★ If the consistency of the buttercream is too wet, sift in 50g (⅓ cup) of icing sugar at a time until it has stiffened up or chill it in the fridge for a short while.

★ A dairy-free alternative for unsalted butter is a baking block. Some brands are vegan but they can taste less buttery. Be mindful that using baking blocks for buttercream in celebration cakes can cause the cake to start melting much faster than real butter, which may compromise its stability and structure.

CHOCOLATE GANACHE

You can use chocolate ganache as a filling alongside buttercream to create an even richer, fudgier flavour in your cakes. It's also perfect for sandwiching between cookies and for filling cookie cups and tempered chocolate shells – try not to finish it off by the spoonful before getting around to adding it to your bakes!

MILK OR DARK CHOCOLATE GANACHE

300g (1¼ cups) double cream, plus extra if needed
600g (20oz) milk or dark chocolate, chopped
Special equipment: Mixer or hand-held electric whisk

Heat the cream in a small saucepan over a low heat until it steams and just starts to bubble. Put the chopped chocolate in a heatproof bowl and pour the hot cream over. Leave the chocolate to melt and gently stir to combine.

Alternatively, put the chocolate and cream in a microwave-proof bowl and heat in 30-second intervals at full power until the chocolate has melted. Use a wooden spoon to mix the chocolate and the cream together.

Ganache should have a thick, silky consistency and can be kept at room temperature for up to 2 days or stored in the fridge for up to 1 month.

To whip it, bring it to room temperature and use the whisk attachment of a mixer (or a hand-held electric whisk) to whip for several minutes until loose and creamy. If the ganache is too stiff, whip in a splash of extra cream or milk, a little at a time. If the ganache is too runny, put it back in the fridge for a while before you whip it again.

WHITE CHOCOLATE GANACHE

200g (¾ cup) double cream, plus extra if needed
600g (20oz) white chocolate, chopped
Special equipment: Mixer or hand-held electric whisk

Follow the method for **MILK OR DARK CHOCOLATE GANACHE** (see left), replacing the milk or dark chocolate with white chocolate and using slightly less double cream – the milk and dark chocolate ganache uses a ratio of 2:1 chocolate to cream, whereas white chocolate ganache uses a ratio of 3:1 chocolate to cream.

FILLINGS

There are hundreds of different fillings you can make or buy to create incredible flavour combinations in your cakes, brownies, cookies and cake jars. Here are some of our favourite – and most commonly requested – fillings. These will come in useful with the recipes in this book.

EDIBLE COOKIE DOUGH

250g (scant 2 cups) plain flour

120g (1 stick) unsalted butter, softened

100g (½ cup) granulated sugar

100g (½ cup packed) light soft brown sugar

2 tsp vanilla extract, or to taste

Pinch of salt

250g (9oz) chocolate chips

Splash of milk, if needed

Special equipment: Mixer or hand-held electric whisk

Preheat the oven to 180°C (160°C fan/350°F/Gas 4). Spread the flour across a baking tray and cook in the oven for 10 minutes (heat-treating the flour is essential for killing bacteria on uncooked flour). Let the flour cool completely, then sift to remove any lumps.

Cream the softened butter and sugars together until combined in a mixer or with a hand-held electric whisk. Add the flour, vanilla extract and salt. Mix in the chocolate chips on a low setting or by hand with a wooden spoon. Add a splash of milk if it is too stiff. Store in the fridge for up to 5 days.

> **TOP TIP**
>
> ★ Add different confectionery, food colourings or extracts for different types of edible cookie dough.

CREAM CHEESE FILLING

180g (6oz) full-fat cream cheese

400g (3⅓ cups) icing sugar, plus extra if needed

2 tbsp cornflour

A dash of lemon juice

Special equipment: Mixer or hand-held electric whisk

Add the cream cheese to a mixer and sift in the icing sugar. Mix on a low speed until combined, then turn it up to medium. It may be quite runny, depending on the brand of icing sugar and the temperature of the cream cheese. Mix in the cornflour to thicken.

If the mixture is still too thin, add more icing sugar, about 50g (⅓ cup) at a time, until the consistency resembles thick royal icing. Add a dash of lemon juice and mix until combined. Store for up to 2 weeks in the fridge.

SALTED CARAMEL

200g (1 cup) granulated sugar
50g (3½ tbsp) unsalted butter, cubed
200ml (scant 1 cup) double cream
1 tsp vanilla extract (optional)
½–1 tsp coarse salt (omit for plain caramel)

Add the sugar to a pan with 50ml (3½ tbsp) water and set over a medium-high heat. Mix until the sugar is dissolved, and wash down any sugar from the sides of the pan using a pastry brush. Once the sugar has dissolved, do not stir again. The water should start to boil, and after 5–6 minutes the sugar mixture will start to turn amber-coloured (the darker the liquid the darker your caramel will be and it can become bitter if left for too long). Do not stir; the pan can be swirled if needed.

Once the mixture is copper-coloured, remove from the heat and add the cubed butter. Whisk to combine. The butter may start to bubble and splutter. Slowly pour in the cream and whisk until the caramel is smooth. Add salt to taste and the vanilla extract, if using. Allow to cool before use; it will thicken as it cools.

For a plain, unsalted caramel, follow the same method without adding salt.

Store in the fridge for up to 7 days.

TOP TIPS ★ Working with sugar is dangerous due to the high temperature it reaches, so please be careful! ★ Use less cream if you require a thicker caramel that solidifies in the fridge.

CREME EGG FILLING

100g (½ cup) caster sugar
100ml (6½ tbsp) water
200g (7oz) white fondant
A few drops of vanilla extract
16ml (1 tbsp) glycerine
Orange gel food colouring

First, make a sugar syrup – these quantities will be enough to make 3 batches: In a pan over a medium heat, bring the caster sugar and water to a simmer, stirring until the sugar has dissolved completely. Bring it to the boil and allow the liquid to become more viscous and reduce down to about 150ml (⅔ cup); this can take up to 10 minutes. Use a wet pastry brush to brush down the sugar caught on the edges of the pan as it cooks. Allow to cool.

Microwave the fondant icing at full power in a microwave-proof bowl for 20–30 seconds. The fondant should be soft and malleable, but not melted. Combine a small amount of the cooled sugar syrup with the warm, soft fondant in a bowl and mix using a wooden spoon – you will need up to 50ml (3½ tbsp) of the sugar syrup, but this depends on the viscosity of the sugar syrup and the softness of the fondant – use a small amount at a time until you have the required consistency. The mixture should turn into a paste.

Add a few drops of vanilla extract to flavour before adding the glycerine. Glycerine helps prevent sugar from crystallizing and adds moisture, so it can help keep it soft and sweet-tasting. It will also add to the authentic shininess of the fondant inside a Creme Egg.

In a separate bowl, add a drop at a time of orange food colouring to a few spoonfuls of the mixture, until you reach the colour desired for the egg yolk. Use the filling as you wish! Store in an air-tight container for up to 2 weeks.

MARSHMALLOW FLUFF FILLING

100ml (6½ tbsp) water

250g (1 cup) golden syrup

150g (⅔ cup) caster sugar, plus 3 heaped tbsp

90g (3oz) egg whites (about 3 egg whites) or
15g (2½ tbsp) dried egg whites

½ tsp cream of tartar

2 tsp vanilla extract

Special equipment: Sugar thermometer,
mixer or hand-held electric whisk

Put the water, golden syrup and 150g (⅔ cup)
caster sugar in a pan ready to start heating.

Put the egg whites and cream of tartar in a clean
metal bowl, and whisk on medium-high speed
until soft peaks form. Alternatively, follow the
instructions on the dried egg powder to make up
the equivalent of 3 egg whites – this will usually
be 1 x 5g (2½ tsp) sachet per egg white.

Heat the sugar, syrup and water mixture over a
medium heat using a sugar thermometer. The
sugar will dissolve and it will start to bubble.

When the egg whites are in-between soft and
stiff peaks, spoon in the 3 heaped tablespoons of
caster sugar, leaving 40 seconds between each
spoonful, and turn the speed up to high. The
mixture should have doubled in size and formed
stiff peaks – when held upright, the mix should
stand up on the end of your whisk.

Once the syrup and sugar liquid has reached
120°C (248°F), take the pan off the heat.

Turn the mixer down to very low. Slowly and
carefully pour in the boiling syrup – make sure
not to pour any liquid on the whisk to avoid
any hot splashes. Add the vanilla extract. Once
incorporated, turn the speed to maximum again
for 5 minutes until the mixture is very thick and
resembles melted marshmallow. Leave to cool
in the bowl before using. Store in the fridge and
eat within 1–2 days.

DULCE DE LECHE FILLING

1 litre (4 cups plus 3 tbsp) full-fat milk

300g (1½ cups packed) light soft brown sugar

2 tsp vanilla extract

Pinch of bicarbonate of soda

Heat the milk in a saucepan, and add the light
soft brown sugar and vanilla extract. Stir well.
Once the milk has started to boil, add a pinch
of bicarbonate of soda. This may start to bubble
but will soon settle. Turn the heat down.

Stir every 5–10 minutes for 1½ hours, making sure
the sauce is not burning. Once it becomes thick
and caramel-like in consistency, stir continuously
for 10–15 minutes. The liquid should have reduced
to a much smaller quantity. Take off the heat and
leave to cool before using. Store in the fridge for
up to 7 days.

PUMPKIN SPICE MIX

6 tbsp sweet ground cinnamon

3 tbsp ground ginger

1 tbsp ground nutmeg

1 tsp allspice

½ tsp ground cloves

Mix the spices together in a bowl. As spices are
very fine, it is easy to add too much allspice or
cloves, which will overpower the mix – try adding
them a pinch at a time, to taste. Store in an
airtight container. Use in our recipes, in coffee
or hot chocolate, or sprinkled over pancakes!

PIPING BAGS & NOZZLES

NOZZLES & COUPLERS

Throughout this book we have used our own branded nozzles, which are named after our amazing team members at Finch Bakery! However, there are plenty of other brands around and they all follow the same universal number system – so any numbered nozzle you see here can be found in various brands.

A coupler is a two-part plastic device that unscrews, allowing a piping nozzle to drop through it and it is then secured to the piping bag when screwed back together. This allows you to change the nozzle without changing the piping bag. A nozzle can be used inside a piping bag with or without a coupler.

PIPING BAGS

There are a variety of different piping bags on the market. Due to ease and hygiene purposes, we use eco-plastic piping bags, however, you may prefer to use washable piping bags that can be reused.

LOADING A PIPING BAG

Place the piping bag in a tall jug or glass with the nozzle pointing downwards, and then roll the piping bag over the sides of the container to expose the nozzle inside. Half-fill the bag – do not fill more than this or it will be too hard to pipe or the bag may split under the pressure. Unfold the sides of the piping bag and twist at the top so that the buttercream stays inside the bag. Snip the end off the piping bag when you're ready to start piping.

HOLDING A PIPING BAG

Holding a piping bag works differently for everyone, just like holding a pencil! One method is to grip the top of the bag from above and clench your fingers and thumb around the bag. Then use your other hand to pincer your forefinger and thumb around the base of the piping bag (near the nozzle) to assist the dominant hand squeezing out the buttercream. However you do it, hold the piping bag vertically initially, and squeeze to get any excess air and buttercream out to prevent spluttering.

MULTI-TONE PIPING

Mixing colours together in a piping bag works well for the first few uses before the colours begin to blend together. Follow these steps to achieve clean colours with multi-tone piping:

For precise lines, put each of your different colours of buttercream into separate piping bags and cut the ends off, ready to pipe.

Place a piece of cling film on a flat work surface and pipe fairly thick lines of each colour directly next to each other in the middle of the cling film. The lines should be a bit shorter than the length of the piping bag. You can also pipe another layer of lines on top, if required.

Carefully roll the cling film into a sausage-shape, keeping the lines intact, and secure each side with a twist. Cut off one of the ends and insert into a piping bag fitted with the desired nozzle.

Pipe as desired and once the buttercream has run out; simply remove the empty cling film and replace with a fresh batch.

PIPING TECHNIQUES

From beautifully piped roses to simple swirls, no matter how they are decorated, cupcakes are still a bestseller in our shop! New piping techniques and nozzles of all shapes and sizes keep cupcakes and celebration cakes on-trend. Good equipment makes all the difference when piping and decorating to ensure a professional-looking result. These piping techniques can also be used on your sheet cakes and tray bakes to create wonderful effects.

CLASSIC ROSETTE

Favourite nozzles: Rachel #2D; Erin #1M
Point the piping bag vertically and, starting in the centre, touch the cupcake with the nozzle. Applying medium pressure, squeeze the piping bag and allow the buttercream to slowly swirl outwards until you reach the edge of the cupcake, and then squeeze and gently pull away to finish.

CLASSIC SWIRL

Favourite nozzles: Erin #1M;
Julie #1B; Kim #1C; Emily #1E
Point the piping bag vertically and, starting at the edge of the cupcake, touch the cupcake with the nozzle. Applying medium pressure, squeeze the piping bag and allow the buttercream to slowly swirl around the edge of the cupcake, working inwards, until you have covered the sponge. Gently squeeze the piping bag and lift away from the cupcake to finish with a small whip on top.

SHELLS

Favourite nozzles: Tessa #348; Erin #1M
Point the piping bag at a 45° angle and touch the sponge at your starting point. Squeeze firmly and allow the shell shape to form, curling upwards before lowering the nozzle downwards. Quickly release and gently pull away. The next shell will cover the last shell's tail. Repeat in a pattern, or around the edge of a cake.

OPEN STAR

Favourite nozzles: Tessa #348; Isabel #9FT
Point the piping bag vertically and touch the cupcake with the nozzle at your starting position. Squeeze gently so that a small star shape appears and then lift the piping bag away from the cupcake; repeat accordingly.

RUFFLES

Favourite nozzles: Lauren #125
Hold the piping bag on its side and make sure the widest part of the triangular nozzle is against the cake and the thinnest part is at the top. Squeeze with medium-firm pressure and the buttercream will come out in a line standing up. Gently zig-zag your hand whilst maintaining the same pressure, then release the pressure and grip to tail the ruffle off.

RUFFLE ROPE

Favourite nozzles: Erin #1M; Rachel #2D; Tessa #348
Hold the piping bag on its side at your starting point and squeeze with medium-firm pressure to form a thick ruffle. Gently zig-zag your hand whilst maintaining the same pressure, guiding the piping bag to create the size of ruffle rope you want, then release the pressure and gently lift the piping bag away.

PIPING A ROSE

Favourites nozzles: Lauren #125 (petal); Hannah #70 (leaf)

Start with the nozzle for the petal. Pipe a cross in the centre of the cupcake – this will help keep the central bud and petals in place.

Holding the piping bag on its side, make sure the widest part of the triangular nozzle is at the bottom against the cake and the thinnest part is at the top. Starting in the centre, slowly pipe a line and twist your hand, holding the cupcake, to allow the line to curl around slightly into a "C" shape. This will be the central bud. Use a cocktail stick to gently push the central bud into the desired position.

Form one petal to tightly encase the central bud by simultaneously squeezing the piping bag, rotating the cupcake and moving the nozzle. Gently pull away the piping bag.

Place the nozzle on the outside of the central bud and petal. Squeeze gently, and move the nozzle in an upside-down "U" shape to create the first petal. Tail off gently. Overlap the petal with the next, repeating the process three times around the central bud to create the next circle of petals. The last petal should overlap the first petal's starting point. If there is ever a build-up of buttercream, use a palette knife to smooth it down towards the cupcake underneath the petals.

Repeat the last step, but pipe five wider petals around the petals you have already piped. The last petal should overlap the first petal's starting point – you will need to rotate the cupcake a total of five times.

Repeat again, but pipe seven even wider petals around the petals you have already piped. The last petal should overlap the first petal's starting point and you will need to rotate the cupcake a total of seven times. Release the pressure and tail off gently. Repeat this process until the full cupcake is covered.

Use the nozzle Hannah #70 to pipe small leaves onto the rose.

You can use these steps on a flower nail and baking parchment, if required. Remove the baking parchment and rose and place in the fridge/freezer until it has crusted over and can be attached to cupcakes or cakes more easily.

FILLING CUPCAKES ★

You can core cupcakes using a coring tool or the end of a large nozzle by inserting it into the sponge and twisting. We prefer to use a teaspoon:

Insert the teaspoon halfway down into the cupcake.

Remove the spoon, rotate it around the cake and repeat three or four times to create a circle that you can scoop out of the middle section.

Fill with your chosen filling and replace the top of cake. Pipe and decorate as required.

TEMPERING CHOCOLATE

There are various specialist techniques that chocolatiers use to temper chocolate, however, we've got some tricks up our sleeves for you, so that anyone can do it.

Every chocolate bar that you buy is already tempered, which is great if you want to eat it – it snaps in your mouth, tastes smooth and won't start melting too quickly when handled. When melted beyond certain temperatures, chocolate loses its temper as the crystals in the cocoa butter begin to misbehave. If left to re-solidify, untempered chocolate will never fully set and will be dull and waxy rather than shiny.

Chocolate with a high percentage of cocoa butter (over 31 per cent for dark chocolate and over 25 per cent for milk chocolate and white chocolate) will give better results and it's better to use more chocolate than needed, as it is easier to control the temperature of higher volumes of chocolate. Surplus chocolate can be spread over a baking sheet and broken up once set to reuse at a later date. If tempering less than 100g (3½oz) of chocolate, halve the times listed here.

MICROWAVE METHOD

This easy method melts already-tempered chocolate so gently that it doesn't come out of its tempered state, and so doesn't need to be re-tempered.

Break the chocolate into small pieces, or use callets (chocolate chips for melting). Put the chocolate into a plastic, microwave-proof bowl (ceramic bowls can heat up quickly, which means it will be more likely for your chocolate to overheat).

Blast the chocolate in the microwave at full power for 1 minute and then stir. The chocolate may not look like it has changed at this stage, but stirring will help distribute the heat throughout the chocolate.

Blast the chocolate for a further 30 seconds. Stir again. The chocolate should start to melt.

Microwave the chocolate at full power for 5–10 seconds at a time (it can be a slow process), stirring each time until there are still just a few lumps left in the chocolate. This is where you should stop heating the chocolate, as the lumps will melt on their own if you continue to stir. If they do not look like they will melt, blast again for another 5 seconds.

TOP TIP ★ You can melt tempered chocolate over a bain marie (a heatproof bowl set over a pan of hot water on the hob), but it is harder to keep the temperature under control. Instead, take the pan off the heat whilst the chocolate melts slowly over it. You can put it back on the heat if the melting slows down.

SEEDING METHOD

This requires melting the chocolate with less precision and re-tempering it by adding in solid already-tempered chocolate at the end. You will need a sugar thermometer for this method.

Break the chocolate up into small pieces, or use callets. Set one-third of the chocolate to the side.

Add 2.5cm (1in) of water to the saucepan and simmer over a low heat. Place a heatproof bowl over the saucepan, making sure no steam can escape. Add two-thirds of the chocolate into the bowl.

Stir the chocolate until completely melted and keep checking the temperature of the chocolate using your thermometer. The chocolate must not reach any higher than the following temperatures:

White chocolate: 43°C (109°F)
Milk chocolate: 46°C (115°F)
Dark chocolate: 48°C (118°F)

Take the bowl off the heat and add in the remaining one-third of the chocolate. The solid chocolate will melt under the heat of the already-melted chocolate, dispersing stable cocoa butter crystals back into the mixture. Keep checking the temperature of your chocolate – it should cool to the following temperatures:

White chocolate: 26°C (79°F)
Milk chocolate: 27°C (81°F)
Dark chocolate: 28°C (82°F)

If you need to improve the fluidity of the chocolate, place the bowl back over the saucepan of warm water to reheat a little (the residual heat will likely be enough to gently warm the chocolate through). The chocolate should reach the following temperatures:

White chocolate: 28°C (82°F)
Milk chocolate: 30°C (86°F)
Dark chocolate: 32°C (90°F)

TOP TIP ★ To test your chocolate, smear a little on a palette knife or a sheet of greaseproof paper. Tempered chocolate should dry quickly, within 4–6 minutes, and will snap nicely when dry.

TEMPERED CHOCOLATE DECORATIONS

To create successful chocolate shards or sails, we recommend first tempering your chocolate in the method of your choice (see pages 30–31) so that it can be handled without melting or bending. If adding colour, use an oil-based food colouring to ensure the chocolate stays fluid and mix it into the chocolate once it is fully melted.

CHOCOLATE SHARDS

Tempered chocolate
Oil-based food colouring (optional)
Sprinkles/decoration (optional)
Special equipment: Baking tray, lined

Colour the tempered chocolate, if you like. Pour the tempered chocolate onto a lined baking tray. Tilt the tray in different directions so that the chocolate spreads evenly or use a palette knife to spread out the chocolate to the desired size. The chocolate should not be too thick – a few millimetres is enough.

Tempered chocolate will start to solidify quickly, so add any toppings, if using. If the topping is hard, such as sprinkles, be aware that you will have to cut the chocolate shard around these which may compromise the shape.

Set aside to harden. For perfectly cut shapes, use a sharp knife to cut the chocolate while still tacky – you can also use metal cutters to form shapes. For irregular shapes, leave the chocolate to fully solidify, then simply break apart with your hands.

CHOCOLATE SHAPES

All kinds of shapes can be made by pouring (or drizzling using a fork or a teaspoon) tempered chocolate onto a lined baking tray. You can also load slightly cooled and thickened chocolate into a piping bag to create more intricate shapes.

CHOCOLATE SAILS

Tempered chocolate
Oil-based food colouring (optional)
Sprinkles/decoration (optional)
Special equipment: Baking tray, lined

Colour the tempered chocolate, if you like. Crumple the baking parchment on the baking tray. Slowly pour on the tempered chocolate; the weight of the chocolate will cause the parchment to flatten slightly. Hold the corners of the paper and tilt in different directions to distribute the chocolate evenly and create unique shapes.

CHOCOLATE BRUSH STROKES

Tempered chocolate
Oil-based food colouring (optional)
Special equipment: Thick paintbrush; baking tray, lined

If using more than one colour, divide the tempered chocolate into separate bowls and colour as required. Dip a thick paintbrush or the back of a spoon into the chocolate and make thin strokes of chocolate on a lined baking tray. The thin chocolate will start to solidify very quickly and the strokes will be fragile once set.

Carefully peel each dried brush stroke off the parchment to decorate as you wish. Use a small blob of melted chocolate or buttercream to stick them to your bake. They look really effective when layered to create a feathered effect.

ASSEMBLING CAKES

Good assembly can make all the difference to the final presentation of your cake. To get a good height on a celebration cake, it's best to bake three or four generous layers in separate tins. You can also bake two deeper cakes and slice each into two layers. These four layers will make an excellent stable foundation for your cake.

LEVELLING & TORTING

Level a cake by cutting the unwanted dome off the top to make it completely flat. Use the cut-offs to make cake jars and cake pops – you can even freeze them for future use.

Torting is when you slice a cake into two or more even layers. This is useful for making two- or four-layer sponges when you are limited on oven space or equipment and the sponges cannot be baked in separate tins.

You can level and torte a cake using a knife to slice through the sponge, although it can be tricky to achieve precise results this way alone. To guide your knife as you slice through the middle, try the "toothpick" method: At 10 or 12 points around the perimeter of the cake, measure halfway up the sponge with a ruler and push in a toothpick (or cocktail stick) about two-thirds of the way in. Remember to remove all the sticks after you're done!

The most precise method is using a cake leveller. More expensive brands, such as Agbay, are sturdy, accurate and use a blade to slice through sponge easily – a must-have for serious bakers, but certainly not essential for home bakers.

Once stacked, you can check your cake using a spirit level – having perfectly level sponges will help create a stable base for any added tiers and decoration.

STACKING A CAKE

Smear a small amount of buttercream or ganache onto a cake board and stick the first layer of cake down.

WITHOUT FILLING: Spoon the desired amount of buttercream or ganache into the centre of the sponge and spread evenly, almost to the edge, with a palette knife. Alternatively, for a more even layer, pipe a circle of buttercream 1cm (½in) from the edge of the sponge. Continue to pipe smaller rings inside the circle until completely filled and smooth over with a palette knife. Stack the next layer on top and repeat the process.

WITH FILLING: Pipe a buttercream or ganache ring 1cm (½in) in from the perimeter on all but one of your sponges. Chill the sponges in the fridge or freezer for 10–15 minutes or until the rings have solidified – these "dams" will act as a barrier to stop softer fillings spilling out over the edges of your cake. Spoon in your filling of choice. Jam and caramel can be quite sticky, so pop the sponges back in the fridge or freezer for another 10 minutes to set before stacking.

For the top layer of your cake, always turn the final sponge layer over so that the level bottom of the sponge becomes the top of the cake. Place the cake in the fridge for 15–20 minutes to set the buttercream before decorating.

DOWELLING

While putting support in a tiered cake is imperative, dowelling a one-tier cake is not always necessary. However, if you are baking in warmer weather or plan to place heavy decoration on top of the cake, it will add internal support to prevent the cake from collapsing. We use jumbo plastic bubble straws for dowelling due to their ease of cutting, affordability and strength, but wooden and plastic dowels are also available, if you prefer.

A good rule to remember is to use 1 dowel per 5cm (2in) of cake, so 4 dowels for a 20cm (8in) cake, for example. If the cake is tall, we'd suggest adding a few more. Dowel your cake once it is firm and set – dowelling a soft cake may result in the layers sliding or the filling spilling out.

Trim your dowels to the height of the cake and push them down vertically into the centre of the sponge, distributing them evenly in a circular pattern around the perimeter of the cake – but not too close to the edge. The dowels should lay flush to the top of the cake.

If you're not adding heavy decoration to the top, carry on decorating as desired. However, if your cake requires support for heavy decoration, secure a thin cake board on top with some buttercream or ganache and pipe over it to cover the cake board before adding decoration. Always remember to let the recipient of the cake know if it contains dowels!

NAKED CAKES

These minimalist-looking cakes have remained a popular request for weddings since we made our first wedding cake (which was a naked one!) in 2013. Different coloured sponges, uneven buttercream application and the ability to hide a multitude of sins with fruit and decoration only adds to the gorgeous rustic appeal and makes these cakes almost foolproof.

WITHOUT FILLING

Sponges such as carrot cake or red velvet do not require a filling.

Follow the method for **STACKING A CAKE - WITHOUT FILLING** (see page 35), but use a piping bag with a star nozzle to pipe the buttercream rings and do not smooth the rings with a palette knife, as you want the pattern to be visible. When stacking each layer, push down gently if the buttercream rings are not visible until they are slightly exposed.

WITH FILLING

Stick the first layer of cake to the cake board with a little buttercream or ganache. Set one sponge aside to use as the top layer and spoon your chosen filling (such as jam or lemon curd) into the centre of the rest of the sponge layers. Use the back of the spoon to spread the filling across the sponges up to the edges – make the filling thinner towards the edges of the cake or it may drip down the sides once stacked. Place these in the fridge for 10–15 minutes for the filling to firm up slightly. Once chilled, follow the stacking process in **NAKED CAKE – WITHOUT FILLING** (see above) to add the buttercream layers, making sure that both the filling and buttercream rings are visible from the outside of the cake.

DECORATING

Naked cakes are often decorated with fruit or flowers, shortbread hearts and a dusting of icing sugar. We sometimes add fruit first and then sift some icing sugar over the top, or hold the cake at an angle to sift icing sugar over the sides of the cake. We've even rolled one in icing sugar! No matter how you finish things off, each naked cake will look completely different to the last one you made.

If using fresh flowers on cakes, make sure that the flowers are free from pesticides, no part of the flower is touching the cake, and florist wire or tape is used before insertion.

CRUMB COATING & APPLYING BUTTERCREAM

Before applying buttercream to a cake, it is often best to crumb coat the cake first. This is the process of covering the outside of the cake with a thin layer of buttercream or ganache to catch excess crumbs before smoothing. It will be partially covered with buttercream with sponge still showing in places.

CRUMB COATING

Load some buttercream on a palette knife and pull it around the edges of the chilled cake, adding more buttercream and roughly smoothing it down until the entire cake is covered. Pile some more buttercream on top of the cake and smooth down to the edges using the palette knife.

Working quickly, use a cake scraper to take off any excess buttercream, and smooth what is left around the sponge. The excess buttercream can be reused, however, there may be some crumbs in the mixture.

Smooth down the ragged edge at the top of the cake using a palette knife, before giving the cake a final once over with the cake scraper. Chill the cake until the buttercream has stiffened up. If any ragged edges still remain, trim them off with a small, sharp knife.

TOP TIP ★ If carefully done, a crumb-coat can be used to achieve a semi-naked finish. Our favourite scraper to use is a metal one, which can be heated using hot water to ensure a really smooth finish. If you are using this technique on your cake as the finished result, it is important that you are extremely careful when covering the sponge with buttercream using a palette knife; crumbs are likely to catch in the buttercream and will be visible on the finished cake.

APPLYING BUTTERCREAM

We like to use a piping bag and cake scraper to achieve a thick, even layer of buttercream over the cake, but you can use a palette knife to spread the buttercream, if you prefer. Make sure your turntable is strong and sturdy or it can shake under the weight of a heavy cake and affect the result.

Crumb coat the cake with buttercream (see left) and chill in the fridge for 10 minutes.

Load buttercream into a piping bag and cut off the end. If the hole is cut too large, the layer of buttercream piped on will be too thick.

Starting at the bottom, pipe even rings of buttercream until the cake is completely covered.

Using a palette knife or scraper, pull the buttercream around the cake and remove the excess until smooth.

You can also use a large, flat piping nozzle (we recommend #789) for a more even application and precision. The buttercream will come out in thin strips so this technique is ideal if you don't want a thick layer of buttercream on the outside of the cake. It can be difficult to ombre colours or to create a multicoloured technique this way, so we'd use this method for a block colour only.

SMOOTHING BUTTERCREAM

USING CAKE SCRAPERS

Cake scrapers are rectangular tools, also known as cake combs, that are used to smooth buttercream or ganache with their straight edges or create elaborate effects with different patterned edges. You can find them made from metal or plastic – both give the same effects but metal ones can be heated under hot water or even a hairdryer (be careful!) to achieve the ultimate smooth finish.

Scrapers are available to buy in many different patterns but depending on the grip of your hand and the pressure applied to the cake, you can even achieve different effects using the same scraper. Patterned scrapers require no more experience than straight-edge scrapers, making them a quick and simple way to give a professional presentation – the technique is the same as the straight-edge scraper.

You can use a straight-edge scraper first to achieve the correct thickness before using the patterned edge. Before using your scraper, check the buttercream is thick enough for the depth of the pattern, as the effect could be compromised if the buttercream is applied too thinly.

Buttercream is more likely to show imperfections if you don't start with the correct consistency, so follow our recipes for perfect buttercream (see page 16) to ensure it isn't too stiff or wet. If you do find the buttercream is a little stiff, just add a few splashes of boiling water from the kettle – we find this smoothes buttercream much more successfully than milk or cold water.

Once the buttercream has been piped on, grip the straight-edge scraper with your fingers across the back and with your thumb gripping the front. Fan your fingers out whilst holding the scraper to apply even pressure.

Hold the scraper at a 45° angle to the cake and smooth the buttercream around the cake. If using a metal scraper, heat it before giving it one final scrape around.

Smooth down the lip of buttercream at the top of the cake with a palette knife before it is chilled, or trim with a sharp knife once chilled.

THE ULTIMATE SMOOTH FINISH

If you are adding a decoration (chocolate drip, piping, sprinkles or leaf), imperfections can be hidden easily, but if the cake requires complete smoothness, the following tips will help:

IF BUBBLES APPEAR IN THE BUTTERCREAM:
Try heating a scraper under a hot tap and giving the cake a once over.

IF THERE IS A LINE LEFT FROM THE SCRAPER:
This can be minimized by very gently pulling the scraper from the cake once finished. Some sort of faint line is inevitable, but if there are quite a few lines, there may be a problem with the balance or sturdiness of your turntable.

IF THE BUTTERCREAM TEARS AWAY FROM THE CAKE: The texture of the buttercream isn't right. Freeze the cake for 20–30 minutes whilst making a new batch of buttercream, and then apply a very thin layer on top. The solid layer will help the newly applied buttercream glide on smoothly.

SCRAPER TECHNIQUES

Using a striped scraper, it is possible to achieve perfect clean stripes quite easily. The trick is to add the first layer of buttercream, then smooth using a striped scraper to create grooves where you will add the other colour, or colours. If you would like a thinner outer layer of buttercream, use less buttercream for the first base coat.

STRIPES TECHNIQUE

Once the buttercream has been applied and smoothed (see pages 39–40), scrape the striped grooves into the cake using a striped scraper.

Chill the cake, ideally in the freezer for 20–30 minutes or the fridge for 45–60 minutes, until the buttercream has hardened.

Using a piping bag, fill in the grooves with the colour(s) of your choice. Working quickly against the cold cake, pull the straight edge of the scraper around the cake to scrape off the excess buttercream. The stripes won't yet be visible, but keep scraping and they'll begin to show through. If you work too slowly, the new buttercream stripes may start solidifying against the first colour, which will be more difficult to scrape off.

You may need to apply different pressure to different parts of the cake in order for all the stripes to be clean and neat; if there are marks on the stripes at the top of the cake, for example, apply more pressure at the top of the cake. Apply firm pressure for best results and don't heat the scraper for this part as the colours may blend together if the buttercream starts to melt.

Smooth the buttercream lip at the top of the cake with a palette knife before chilling or trim with a small sharp knife once chilled. Your stripy cake will be ready to decorate after chilling in the fridge for a further 10–15 minutes.

RAINBOW STRIPES TECHNIQUE

Start with a crumb-coated cake (see page 39). Check how many stripes you will make by holding the scraper against the cake and counting how many grooves fit.

Divide the buttercream into separate bowls for the number of colours you require. Mix each bowl to the desired colour and then load each colour into a separate piping bag. Lay your piping bags in your chosen colour order.

Using the striped scraper, score stripes onto the cake, pressing hard to enable visible guidelines. The scraper will carve away buttercream and create grooves within the crumb coat. Pipe the buttercream colours onto the raised ridges (leave the grooves plain for now).

Heat the scraper if needed and use the striped edge at a 45° angle to smooth down the piped buttercream. The first colours should now appear as stripes – don't worry if colours have blended together in the indentation grooves at this point.

Chill the cake, ideally in the freezer for 20–30 minutes or in the fridge for 45–60 minutes, until the buttercream has hardened slightly.

Pipe the grooves with the remaining colours and pull the straight edge of the scraper around the cake to smooth and scrape off the excess buttercream. Apply very firm pressure. Don't heat the scraper for this stage or the colours may blend together.

FAULT LINE TECHNIQUE

This trend has emerged in the cake decorating world over the past few years. You can decorate the exposed section with anything you like – a different coloured buttercream, another pattern, confectionery and even sprinkles.

Apply and smooth your first layer of buttercream (see pages 39–40). This will be the exposed part of the cake. If this section requires a different pattern, use the desired patterned scraper at this stage, working only on the part that will remain exposed. If your design requires something like sprinkles, work quickly and press them in while the buttercream is soft. Once complete, chill the cake in the fridge for 45–60 minutes, until this first layer is set.

Once chilled, use a palette knife or piping bag to apply the buttercream for your fault line to the bottom section of the cake in thick strips. Make sure it is applied thicker than the first layer and just reaches the edges of the exposed section – this will ensure that the design you want to show in the exposed section won't get fully covered or damaged when you are smoothing down the outer layer of buttercream.

Use a patterned scraper or a palette knife to smooth down the strips of buttercream, avoiding the exposed section. This is not supposed to be neat – the edges should be ragged, like a fault line! We've gone with a zig-zag scraper here.

Once you've perfected this technique, why not try a full, double fault line, by adding a buttercream fault line layer to the top section of the cake too, so that only the middle section remains exposed. As your skills grow, you can even try a vertical fault line!

RUFFLES TECHNIQUE

Romantic ruffles are still one of the most popular designs we get asked to create on wedding cakes. You can use a palette knife to achieve this effect in minutes and it is an easy way to add a rustic feel to a wedding cake. Team with fruit or flowers for a simplistic but stunning centrepiece. The size of the palette knife will determine the texture – if the end of the palette knife is narrow, it will create a much tighter ruffle than a wider palette knife.

Apply and smooth your buttercream (see pages 39–40), but do not chill the cake before the next step.

Heat a palette knife by dipping it into a jug of just-boiled water, then wipe dry with a tea towel. Starting at the bottom of the cake, place the palette knife on the buttercream and press down gently. Start turning the turntable with one hand whilst making grooves with the palette knife with the other. Try to make one continuous line.

Once there is one complete ring around the cake, move upwards and repeat. The trick is to try and get neat and even grooves; the lip in-between each ring will act as the ruffle. Don't worry if it's not perfect – this will add to the rustic appeal!

OMBRE TECHNIQUE

Ombre is not just a trend in hairdressing, it's a popular technique in the cake decorating world, too! Applying colours on the cake in a gradient of shades or blending completely different colours together is quite easy and effective to achieve.

Make your buttercream in the colours and flavours required (see pages 16–17). Apply the buttercream (see page 39) in thick strips for each colour, working from the top down. There will be an evident split in each colour at this point.

If you want the colours to slightly merge together, run a palette knife around where each section meets to blend and soften the harsh lines. Use a straight-edge scraper to smooth down and scrape off the excess buttercream (see page 40).

Smooth down the buttercream again using a straight-edge or patterned cake scraper (patterned scrapers can be quite forgiving they help to conceal harsher lines). If using metal equipment, heat the scraper before giving it one final scrape for an extra smooth finish.

Use a palette knife to smooth down the buttercream lip at the top of the cake before it is chilled, or trim with a sharp knife once chilled.

WATERCOLOUR TECHNIQUE

Watercolour technique in buttercream works really well with lighter colours – think pales and pastels. It's a simple technique with no set rules to follow, and is likely to end with a different result every time. When incorporating dark colours with lighter colours, make sure there is only a very small amount of the darker colour as it can overpower the paler ones.

Make your buttercream in the colours and flavours required (see pages 16–17). Apply the buttercream (see page 39), piping even blobs to cover the entire sides of the cake.

Use a straight-edge scraper to smooth down (see page 40) and scrape off the excess buttercream. The colours should naturally blend together, and the excess buttercream (there may be lots of it!) can be used to decorate the rest of the cake or saved for another bake.

Smooth down the buttercream again using a straight-edge or textured cake scraper of your choosing – textured scrapers (think bubble or zig-zag) can enhance the watercolour effect. If using metal equipment, heat the scraper before giving it one final scrape for an extra smooth finish.

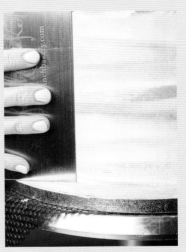

OIL PAINTING TECHNIQUE

This technique doesn't follow any rules. Adding texture to your cake is easy and every design will end up unique. You can use this technique to hide a multitude of sins on smooth buttercream and the results can be quite striking! Perfect for a wedding cake.

Apply a light buttercream base (see page 39) – we generally choose white as the other colours added will stand out more against the lighter base.

Smooth down your cake (see page 40) – if your painted section is a focal point, you may want a smoother base, if it is all over, the smoothness shouldn't matter.

Chill the cake in the fridge for 20–30 minutes to allow the base layer to start solidifying.

Depending on your design, use a palette knife to build up colours in certain sections of the cake, smearing strokes of coloured buttercream in different directions. If it's easier, pipe blobs of buttercream directly onto the cake before smearing with a palette knife.

Occasionally scrape around the cake with a straight-edge scraper to smooth and blend colours together – there should be a few different layers of colour building up.

To finish with a smooth look, scrape around the cake one final time, or, for a textured look, finish with a few strokes of buttercream from your palette knife. Using a small palette knife, you can even create abstract petals and flowers using gentle strokes.

DRIP TECHNIQUES

The drip effect is a popular choice of decoration and gives the perfect touch to a buttercream cake. There are several different ways you can make a drip for your cake, depending on the desired look, timescale and level of skill required. When adding colour to chocolate, always use an oil-based food colouring as a water or gel-based food colouring will cause the chocolate to seize.

These recipes make enough to cover a 20cm (8in) cake.

CHOCOLATE SPREAD DRIP

100g (½ cup) white chocolate spread
Oil-based food colouring (optional)
Sprinkles/decorations (optional)

The secret ingredient we use on most of our celebration cakes is supermarket own-brand chocolate spread. Some branded chocolate spreads tend to stay thick even when melted, so don't achieve as smooth a drip. If adding colour, start with a white chocolate spread. Most chocolate spreads contain hazelnuts so be sure to check for allergies before using.

Spoon the spread into a microwave-proof bowl or jug. Microwave at full power for 10 seconds at a time until fully melted. Leave the melted spread for a few minutes – until cool but still liquid – this will stop the buttercream on your cake melting and thicken up the spread slightly.

If using food colouring, put one drop at a time into the melted spread and mix, slowly adding more to achieve the desired shade.

With a teaspoon, carefully pool a small amount of the drip mixture on top of the cake, near the edge. Use the spoon to push the spread from the top of the cake over the edge, creating drips in different lengths. The spread will remain tacky rather than drying solid, which is perfect for pushing in individual sprinkles to create an extra special finish. Be careful not to smudge the drips!

MELTED CHOCOLATE DRIP

100g (3½oz) white chocolate chips, for melting
1 tsp vegetable oil
Oil-based food colouring (optional)
Sprinkles/decorations (optional)

Another easy way of creating a drip is by combining melted chocolate with vegetable oil. We find this makes the chocolate much smoother, making it perfect to drip down the cake yet still drying relatively hard, which is ideal to use when painting with lustre dust for a metallic drip. This method can be used with white, milk and dark chocolate. If the quality of the chocolate is high, the chocolate drip may not even require any oil.

Melt the chocolate in the microwave at full power for 1 minute and then at 5-second intervals until fully melted. Add the vegetable oil and mix. If you want to colour the drip, add the oil-based food colouring at this point.

Use a teaspoon to carefully pool a small amount of the melted chocolate on the top of the cake, near the edge, and gently push the mixture over the edge to create drips in different lengths.

These chocolate drips will dry hard – the more vegetable oil that is added, the thinner the drips will be and more tacky the chocolate will become, enabling you to add sprinkles and decorations, if desired.

CHOCOLATE GANACHE DRIP

100g (3½oz) white chocolate chips, for melting

50ml (3½ tbsp) double cream, plus an extra 1–2 tsp

Oil-based food colouring (optional)

This is probably the most popular way to achieve a drip for a cake. There are differing opinions of how to add the chocolate and the cream, but we find that melting them together creates the best consistency. This technique can be tricky to master as ganache is easy to split – if the mixture is too thick, the drips can look lumpy and if it is too thin, it can run down the cake too easily and become transparent.

Using a 2:1 ratio of white chocolate to double cream, heat together in the microwave at full power for 1 minute at a time until fully melted, then mix. If required, you can also melt on a low heat in a pan on the hob.

Stir the ganache and leave to cool slightly so that it is still liquid but not so hot that it will melt the buttercream on your cake. The ganache should be thick but still thin enough to flow off the spoon. If needed, add an extra 1–2 teaspoons of double cream and stir until combined. If using, mix in the oil-based food colouring one drop at a time to achieve your desired colour.

Using a teaspoon, carefully spoon some of the ganache and pool a small amount on top of the cake, near the edge. With the spoon, gently nudge the mixture from the top of the cake over the edge to create drips of different lengths.

The state of ganache once dry will depend on the amount of cream that was added – the more white chocolate that the ganache contains, the harder the drip will dry.

CARAMEL DRIP

A caramel drip is perfect for sticky toffee pudding and other caramel-themed cakes. Caramel can be bought in jars ready to use but if you want to make it from scratch, follow the **SALTED CARAMEL** recipe on page 21 (leave the salt out if you prefer a plain caramel) and allow it to cool before using. Melt in a couple of squares of white chocolate whilst heating the caramel to help the drip firm up and stay in place all day. Caramel drips will never set hard, however, you should be able to add light sprinkles without affecting the shape of the drip.

UPSIDE-DOWN DRIP

The upside-down drip is an effective way to add a drip to a cake with a difference - gravity defying! The process is a simple one: create drips using your chosen method and allow them to set, then flip the cake upside-down! We recommend sandwiching the cake between two cakeboards to turn it over fairly easily.

TOP TIPS

★ These mixtures can also be loaded into a squeezy bottle to use with more accuracy, if preferred.

★ Add sprinkles to the drip by using tweezers or wetting your finger and pressing it into some sprinkles, then carefully onto the individual drips.

★ Make sure the drips are dry before decorating the top of the cake - we recommend putting it back in the fridge to chill for 30 minutes.

HALF & HALF CAKE

One of the showstoppers born in our bakery... the half and half cake! It's most often requested for shared birthdays, but if you just can't decide between your two favourite flavours, why not have both! This method shows you how to assemble the cake – you can choose any flavours you like for it.

INGREDIENTS

4 even layers of cake sponge (2 layers of each flavour)
2 batches of buttercream (1 batch of each flavour)
Fillings (optional; 1 filling for each flavour)
Special equipment: Piping bags, cake drum

Cut all four sponges in half to create eight semicircles. Set one semicircle of each flavour aside – these will be the top ones.

Smear a little buttercream onto the cake drum to fix one semicircle of each flavour, piping a line of buttercream between the two sponge halves to secure them together and create the base layer.

Pipe a buttercream dam around the perimeters of the sponges (except the top ones) in the chosen flavour for each. If the buttercream is too soft, chill the sponges in the fridge or freezer for 15 minutes to help the dams solidify – this will help to stop any filling overspill later on. Fill the buttercream dams with your chosen fillings, if using, and buttercream. Chill the sponges in the fridge for 10 minutes before stacking the cake.

You can add the fillings as you stack the cake but we find that chilling the already filled sponges and then stacking often saves time and helps to set the fillings to prevent overspill and improve the stability of the cake.

Once neatly stacked, pipe a line of buttercream along the middle of the cake over where the two halves meet and use a palette knife to roughly smooth down and conceal any gaps between the two halves. Crumb coat (see page 39) the cake to secure the sponges together.

Apply your chosen buttercream (see page 39) to one half of the cake. Blend the edges slightly into the half that is still crumb-coated – hold the scraper and pull it backwards to smooth down and make the layer a little thinner towards the crumb-coated side. Place the cake in the fridge for 45 minutes or in the freezer for 20 minutes, or until the buttercream has solidified.

Use two pieces of baking parchment as a stencil to create a straight line at each side where the second flavour of buttercream will meet the half that is already applied.

Carefully and evenly apply the second flavour of buttercream on the opposite side of the cake. Make sure not to press too hard when applying it over the baking parchment so that the buttercream underneath is not damaged.

Smooth the buttercream using a straight-edge scraper, scraping away any excess and only going lightly over where the parchment is. Use a heated metal scraper for a smooth finish or add a pattern from a textured scraper, if you wish.

Carefully pull both sheets of baking parchment from the cake to reveal a straight line between the two flavours. If there is a lip of buttercream at the top of the cake, smooth it down with a palette knife before chilling or trim with a sharp knife once chilled.

Decorate as you wish – we love using half white chocolate and half milk chocolate, or different colours on both sides for a truly spectacular half and half effect!

CAKE JAR TUTORIAL

These beauties are one of the things that initially put our little bakery on the map! Layering sponge inside a jar creates an impressive mess-free dessert – just grab a spoon and you're ready to go. Our customers have taken their cake jars to the cinema, on hikes and even abroad... what could be better than indulging in a cake jar on the beach!

Cake jars are perfect for using up leftover buttercream and cupcakes or cake cut-offs. This method shows you how to make cake jars with already-baked sponge – generally, each layer of sponge requires 50g (1¾oz) of cake (or 1 cupcake). Our cake jar recipes fill a standard 454g (1lb) jam jar.

You can add as many layers and fillings as you like to your cake jars... sponge and buttercream only, or fillings such as jam, lemon curd, caramel, ganache or chocolate spread. Add a little extra buttercream for flavours that need no additional filling, such as carrot cake and red velvet.

INGREDIENTS

Makes 4 cake jars

Buttercream as specified in individual recipe

600g (21oz) cake (around 12 cupcakes)

Fillings as specified in individual recipe (optional)

SPECIAL EQUIPMENT

Piping bags and nozzle of your choice (optional)

4 x 454g (1lb) jam jars

> **TOP TIP** ★ If you are using a spread such as Nutella or Lotus Biscoff as the filling, melt it in the microwave and pour on top of the sponge for each layer. Tilt and rotate the jar in your hand so that the melted spread covers the sponge evenly and is visible from the outside of the jar. Allow to cool slightly before piping the buttercream on top of the spread, or it may melt.

1 Load the buttercream into a piping bag and snip 1cm (⅜in) from the tip (you can use a nozzle, if you like). Pipe a blob of buttercream into the bottom of a jar.

2 Crumble 50g (1¾oz) of cake or 1 cupcake into the bottom of the jar. Lightly push down and flatten the cake using the end of a rolling pin.

3 Load any filling, if using, into another piping bag and pipe a ring around the perimeter of the jar. Alternatively, spoon filling into the jar and use the back of the spoon to spread it in a thin layer.

4 Pipe a ring of buttercream around the perimeter of the jar, on top of the filling.

5 Repeat with another layer of cake, any fillings (if using) and buttercream. The general rule is to add 1 teaspoon of filling per layer.

6 Add a third layer of cake and finish by squeezing a small blob of filling (if using) in the middle and piping a final ring of buttercream.

7 If you have the willpower to resist eating it straight away, screw the lid on to enjoy it later. Cake jars will keep for 3 days; cake jars that include cream or cream cheese are best eaten on the day you make them or should be stored in the fridge.

CELEBRATION CAKES, CUPCAKES & CAKE JARS

CLASSIC VICTORIA SPONGE

This classic recipe is easy to make with delicious results. A light sponge and sweet buttercream is complemented with raspberry or strawberry jam. For a quintessentially British afternoon tea or to cut into a big triangular wedge on your birthday, we are sure you will find an excuse to whip up this cake!

INGREDIENTS

Makes a 20cm (8in), 4-layer cake

600g (5 sticks) unsalted butter

600g (3 cups) caster sugar

10 eggs

600g (4⅔ cups) self-raising flour

Vanilla buttercream

250g (2 sticks) unsalted butter

500g (3½ cups) icing sugar

Vanilla extract, to taste

Filling

About 150g (½ cup) strawberry or raspberry jam

Decoration

750g (6 sticks plus 2 tbsp) unsalted butter

1.5kg (8¼ cups) icing sugar

Vanilla extract, to taste

15g (4 tsp) whitening powder (optional)

Pink gel food colouring

Geo-heart Cake Shapes and Cakesicles (see pages 204–206)

White chocolate spread

Pink oil-based food colouring

Sprinkles and edible glitter

SPECIAL EQUIPMENT

Mixer or hand-held electric whisk

4 x 20cm (8in) cake tins, lined

Cake drum, turntable and dowels (optional)

Piping bags and Erin #1M nozzle (or nozzle of choice)

Straight-edge and zig-zag scraper

Sphere and cakesicle moulds

1   Preheat the oven to 180°C (160°C fan/350°F/Gas 4).

2   Put the butter and sugar into a mixer and, using the paddle attachment, cream together on a high speed (or use a hand-held electric whisk).

3   When the butter and sugar are combined and the butter has changed to a paler colour, turn the mixer speed down to medium. Add the eggs, one by one, until combined.

4   Sift in the flour and fold in using a spatula, or combine using a low-speed setting. Do not overmix.

5   Evenly divide the batter among the four lined tins; 500g (18oz) into each. Bake in the preheated oven for 30–35 minutes, or until the sponge bounces back when pressed. You can also check by inserting a toothpick into the centre; if it comes out clean, the cake is ready.

6   Let them cool for 5–10 minutes in the tins, then carefully turn out the cakes onto wire racks and leave until completely cold.

Filling and stacking

7   Make a batch of **VANILLA BUTTERCREAM** (see page 16), adding the vanilla extract to taste.

8   Level and stack the cake (see pages 34–35), using strawberry or raspberry jam and the vanilla buttercream for the fillings.

9   Dowel the cake using the method on page 35 (optional).

10   Chill the cake in the fridge for 30 minutes until the buttercream has solidified. Crumb coat the cake (see page 39) with the remaining buttercream. Chill for 30 minutes or until you are ready to decorate. ▶

Decoration

11 Make a large batch of **VANILLA BUTTERCREAM** using the butter, icing sugar and vanilla extract (see page 16 for method). Sift and mix in the whitening powder, if using. Set one-third of the batch aside for piping the rosettes.

12 Put a couple of scoops of buttercream into a piping bag and mix in a touch of pink gel food colouring to what's left in the bowl to create a pale pink colour; add a couple of scoops of this to another piping bag. Repeat to continue creating deeper shades of pink (you can do as many or as few as you want) until all the buttercream is coloured and in several piping bags.

13 Place the cake on your turntable and apply the pink buttercreams using the watercolour technique (see page 47), finishing the effect using a zig-zag scraper. Chill the cake for 10–15 minutes or until you are ready to decorate.

14 Mix any excess buttercream from the piping bags and scraping the cake, with the buttercream batch for the rosettes. Add a little more food colouring, if you like.

15 Make the **GEO-HEART CAKE SHAPES** and **CAKESICLES** (see pages 204–206) – these can also be made in advance and stored in the fridge until needed.

16 Add a drip of your choice (see page 50) – we used white chocolate spread, coloured pink with oil-based food colouring.

17 Load the buttercream into a piping bag fitted with your nozzle of choice. Pipe small rosettes (see page 26) around the perimeter of the cake. Fill in the middle of the cake with more rosettes and around the base covering the cake board.

18 Decorate the rosettes with a scatter of sprinkles. Arrange the cakesicles and geo-hearts on the cake. We also included a mini chocolate sail (see page 32), tempered chocolate spheres (see page 198) and some gold leaf (see page 15) across the drip.

19 Chill in the fridge for a couple of hours, or until the day you are cutting the cake.

VANILLA CUPCAKES & JARS

INGREDIENTS

Makes 12 cupcakes / 4 cake jars

180g (1½ sticks) unsalted butter

180g (¾ cup plus 2 tbsp) caster sugar

180g (1½ cups) self-raising flour

3 eggs

Vanilla buttercream

150g (1 stick plus 2 tbsp) unsalted butter

300g (2 cups plus 2 tbsp) icing sugar

Vanilla extract, to taste

5g (½ tsp) whitening powder (optional)

Pink gel food colouring

Filling

200g (7oz) strawberry or raspberry jam

Decoration

Sprinkles and edible glitter

SPECIAL EQUIPMENT

Mixer or hand-held electric whisk

12-hole cupcake tin, lined with cases

Piping bag and Erin #1M nozzle (or nozzle of choice)

1 Use the quantities listed here for the butter, caster sugar, self-raising flour and eggs to make the cake batter (see steps 1–4 on page 59 for method), and divide it between the cupcake cases until just over half-filled. Bake for 15–20 minutes, then cool completely on a wire rack.

2 Make a batch of **VANILLA BUTTERCREAM** (see page 16 for method) using the butter, icing sugar, vanilla extract to taste and whitening powder, if using. Separate the buttercream into three bowls. Colour two of the bowls different shades of pink.

3 Core and fill the cupcakes (see page 29) using strawberry or raspberry jam.

4 Load the buttercream into a piping bag fitted with your nozzle of choice using the multi-tone piping method (see page 24) and pipe the cupcakes in a classic rosette (see page 26). Decorate with sprinkles and edible glitter.

To make cake jars

If you are making fresh sponge and buttercream for your jars, follow step 1 of the method above to make 12 vanilla cupcakes and step 2 to make the vanilla buttercream – colour it if you like.

You will need 3 cupcakes or 150g (5oz) of cake per jar. Allow 50g (1¾oz) of strawberry or raspberry jam per cake jar.

Fill the jars in layers following the cake jar tutorial on page 55.

INGREDIENTS

Makes a 20cm (8in), 5-layer cake

- 250g (2 sticks) unsalted butter
- 250ml (1 cup) vegetable oil
- 10 eggs
- 1 tsp vanilla extract
- 500g (2½ cups packed) light soft brown sugar
- 375g (scant 2 cups) caster sugar
- 150g (1½ cups) cocoa powder
- ½ tsp salt
- 2 tsp fine instant coffee
- 750ml (3 cups) boiling water
- 625g (4¾ cups) plain flour
- 1 tsp bicarbonate of soda
- 1 tbsp baking powder

Chocolate buttercream

- 250g (2 sticks) unsalted butter
- 450g (3¼ cups) icing sugar
- 50g (½ cup) cocoa powder
- Pinch of salt

Milk or dark chocolate ganache

- 400g (14oz) milk or dark chocolate
- 200ml (scant 1 cup) double cream

Decoration

- 500g (4 sticks plus 2 tbsp) unsalted butter
- 900g (7½ cups) icing sugar
- 100g (1 cup) cocoa powder, plus extra to create the darker shade
- Chocolate shards (see page 32), sprinkles, gold leaf and chocolates

SPECIAL EQUIPMENT

Mixer or hand-held electric whisk

5 x 20cm (8in) cake tins, lined

28cm (11in) cake drum, turntable and dowels

Piping bag and Erin #1M nozzle (or nozzle of choice)

Medium stripe cake scraper

CHOCOLATE FUDGE CAKE

Indulgent and decadent, this chocolate cake uses oil and butter in equal parts, keeping the sponge light and bouncy yet satisfyingly rich and fudgy. A Finch Bakery classic.

1 Preheat the oven to 180°C (160°C fan/350°F/Gas 4).

2 Melt the butter in the microwave at full power or in a pan over a low heat.

3 Add the vegetable oil to the mixer bowl with the eggs, vanilla extract, light soft brown sugar, caster sugar and melted butter, and beat for 4–5 minutes. Alternatively, use a mixing bowl and hand-held electric whisk.

4 Place the cocoa powder, salt and instant coffee into another bowl with the boiling water and mix until smooth. Pour this liquid into the first bowl and combine.

5 Sift the flour into a third bowl along with the bicarbonate of soda and baking powder. Spoon the dry ingredients into the wet mixture slowly, folding in using a spatula or using a low setting on the mixer. Do not overmix.

6 Divide the batter equally among the lined tins. Bake in the oven for 30–35 minutes, or until the sponge bounces back when pressed. You can also check by inserting a sharp knife into the centre; if it comes out clean, the cake is ready.

7 Allow to cool in the tins for 5–10 minutes, then carefully turn out onto wire racks and leave to cool completely.

Filling and stacking

8 Make a batch of **CHOCOLATE BUTTERCREAM** (see page 16) and some **MILK OR DARK CHOCOLATE GANACHE** (see page 19) using the quantities listed here.

9 Level, stack and dowel the cake following the instructions on pages 34–35 for a cake with filling. Reserve some ganache for the chocolate drip. ▶

10 Chill the cake for 30 minutes until the buttercream has solidified, then follow the crumb coating method on page 39, with the remaining buttercream. Chill the cake for 30 minutes or until you are ready to decorate.

Decoration

11 Make a large batch of **CHOCOLATE BUTTERCREAM** (see page 16 for method) using the quantities on page 63 for the butter, icing sugar and cocoa powder – save any leftover for cake jars!

12 Take the cake out of the fridge and place onto a turntable. Apply and smooth the buttercream base (see pages 39–40), then follow the striped buttercream technique on page 43. Once the first colour has been piped onto the cake, mix a little more cocoa powder in the remaining buttercream to turn it a darker shade for the second stripe colour.

13 Put any leftover buttercream from the piping bags, or that you have scraped off the cake, into a bowl and set aside.

14 Whilst waiting for the cake to set, make some chocolate shards (see page 32) and select the chocolate or decoration that you are going to use on top of the cake.

15 Prepare your preferred drip method (see page 50). For this cake, we used milk chocolate ganache. If the ganache starts to solidify, heat it in the microwave at full power in short bursts until runny again. Using a spoon, apply the ganache across the top of the cake and to the edge, and then allow it to drip down the cake.

16 Load a piping bag fitted with your nozzle of choice with the excess buttercream, and pipe small whips around the perimeter of the cake at the top and bottom.

17 Decorate with sprinkles, chocolate shards and chocolates. We have also applied gold leaf (see page 15) across the drip.

18 Chill in the fridge for a couple of hours, or until the day you are cutting the cake.

CHOCOLATE FUDGE CUPCAKES & JARS

INGREDIENTS

Makes 12 cupcakes / 4 cake jars

70g (5 tbsp) unsalted butter

70ml (5 tbsp) vegetable oil

3 eggs

1 tsp vanilla extract

135g (⅔ cup packed) light soft brown sugar

100g (½ cup) caster sugar

50g (½ cup) cocoa powder

¼ tsp salt

½ tsp fine instant coffee

200ml (scant 1 cup) boiling water

170g (1⅓ cups) plain flour

¼ tsp bicarbonate of soda

1 tsp baking powder

Milk or dark chocolate ganache

65g (2¼oz) milk or dark chocolate

130ml (scant ⅔ cup) double cream

Chocolate whipped cream buttercream

110g (7½ tbsp) unsalted butter

220g (1¾ cups) icing sugar

30g (⅓ cup) cocoa powder

50ml (3½ tbsp) double cream

Decoration

12 Flake pieces (optional)

SPECIAL EQUIPMENT

Mixer or hand-held electric whisk

12-hole cupcake tin, lined with cases

Piping bag and Erin #1M nozzle (or nozzle of choice)

1 Using the quantities listed here, follow steps 1–5 of the **CHOCOLATE FUDGE CAKE** method (see page 63) to make the cake batter. Divide the batter between the cupcake cases, filling them around three-quarters full.

2 Bake in the oven for 20–22 minutes, or until the cupcakes spring back when pressed. Transfer to a wire rack to cool.

3 Prepare a batch of **MILK OR DARK CHOCOLATE GANACHE** (see page 19) using the quantities listed here. Core and fill the cupcakes (see page 29) using some of the ganache.

4 Prepare a batch of **CHOCOLATE WHIPPED CREAM BUTTERCREAM** (see page 17) using the quantities given here. Load a piping bag with your preferred nozzle and decorate the cupcakes with your chosen techniques (see pages 26–29).

5 Drizzle the remaining ganache over the cupcakes and top each one with a piece of Flake, if using.

To make cake jars

If you are making fresh sponge and buttercream for your cake jars, follow the method above to make 12 chocolate fudge cupcakes (undecorated), the chocolate buttercream and the ganache.

For the ganache, you will need to use 150g (5oz) milk or dark chocolate and 75ml (⅓ cup) double cream to allow 50g (1¾oz) of chocolate ganache per cake jar.

You will need 3 cupcakes or 150g (5oz) of cake per jar.

Fill the jars in layers following the cake jar tutorial on page 55.

FUNFETTI LAYER CAKE

Light, fluffy and filled with rainbow sprinkles, this fun sponge cake makes the perfect celebration cake, cupcakes and jars with a range of brightly coloured fillings. Cut your cake open to reveal little rainbow dots peppered throughout!

INGREDIENTS

Makes a 20cm (8in), 4-layer cake

600g (5 sticks) unsalted butter

600g (3 cups) caster sugar

10 eggs

600g (4⅔ cups) self-raising flour

170–250g (6–9oz) bake-stable funfetti sprinkles

Whipped cream buttercream

250g (2 sticks) unsalted butter

500g (3½ cups) icing sugar

100ml (6½ tbsp) double cream

250g (9oz) white chocolate

Pinch of salt

Decoration

500g (4 sticks plus 2 tbsp) unsalted butter

1kg (7 cups) icing sugar

Vanilla extract, to taste

15g (4 tsp) whitening powder (optional)

Pink, orange, yellow, green, blue and purple gel food colourings

White chocolate spread

Pink oil-based food colouring

Sprinkles, edible silver glitter, sweets and lollipops
(we use Walkston Candy)

SPECIAL EQUIPMENT

Mixer or hand-held electric whisk

4 x 20cm (8in) cake tins, lined

Cake drum, turntable and dowels (optional)

Straight-edge and striped scraper

Piping bags and Erin #1M nozzle (or nozzle of choice)

1 Follow steps 1–6 of the **CLASSIC VICTORIA SPONGE** method on page 59, adding the bake-stable funfetti sprinkles into the batter during step 4.

Filling and stacking

2 Make a batch of **WHIPPED CREAM BUTTERCREAM** (see page 17) using the quantities listed here.

3 Level and stack the cake following the instructions on pages 34–35. Dowel the cake using the method on page 35 (optional). Chill the cake in the fridge for 30 minutes until the buttercream has solidified.

4 Crumb coat the cake (see page 39) with the remaining buttercream and chill for further 30 minutes or until ready to decorate.

Decoration

5 Make a batch of **VANILLA BUTTERCREAM** using the quantities listed here for the butter, icing sugar, vanilla extract and whitening powder, if using (see page 16 for method).

6 Apply and smooth the buttercream (see pages 39–40), then use the striped scraper to create grooves in the buttercream, around the cake. Chill the cake, ideally in the freezer for 20–30 minutes or the fridge for 45–60 minutes, until the buttercream has hardened.

7 While the cake is chilling, put 3 tablespoons each of the white buttercream into seven small bowls. Use the gel food colourings to colour each one a different shade – add just a little for pastel shades. For this cake, we used dark pink, light pink, orange, yellow, green, blue and purple. Set the bowls in the order you will use the colours. ▶

8 Load a piping bag with each colour, keeping the bags in the correct colour order. Pipe each of your colours into the grooves of the cake in your chosen order.

9 Working quickly against the cold cake, pull the straight edge of the scraper around the cake to scrape off the excess buttercream. The stripes won't yet be visible, but keep scraping and they'll begin to show through. If you work too slowly, the new buttercream stripes may start solidifying against the first colour, which will be more difficult to scrape off. See the full method for the stripes technique on page 45 and follow the tips to achieve a perfect striped finish.

10 Add a drip of your choice (see page 50) – we used white chocolate spread, coloured pink with oil-based food colouring. Chill for 15 minutes until the drip has solidified. Add sprinkles to the drip while it is still tacky, as well as to the sides of the cake – use a clean finger to gently pat on the sprinkles while the buttercream is still soft, or use a fine paintbrush to add a little water to help the sprinkles stick.

11 Load a piping bag with your nozzle of choice and the remaining white buttercream. Pipe small rosettes (see page 26) around the perimeter of the cake. Fill in the middle of the cake with more rosettes and around the base to cover the cake drum.

12 Decorate with edible silver glitter, colourful sweets and lollipops.

13 Chill in the fridge for a couple of hours, or until the day you are cutting the cake.

FUNFETTI CUPCAKES & JARS

INGREDIENTS

Makes 12 cupcakes / 4 cake jars

180g (1½ sticks) unsalted butter

180g (¾ cup plus 2 tbsp) caster sugar

180g (1½ cups) self-raising flour

3 eggs

40g (about 1½oz) bake-stable funfetti sprinkles

Whipped cream buttercream

125g (1 stick) unsalted butter

250g (1¾ cups) icing sugar

50ml (3½ tbsp) double cream

125g (4oz) white chocolate

Pink, orange, yellow, green, blue and purple gel food colourings

Decoration

Sprinkles, sweets and edible glitter

SPECIAL EQUIPMENT

Mixer or hand-held electric whisk

12-hole cupcake tin, lined with cases

Piping bag and Erin #1M nozzle (or nozzle of choice)

1 Preheat the oven to 180°C (160°C fan/350°F/Gas 4).

2 Use the quantities listed here for the butter, caster sugar, self-raising flour, eggs and funfetti sprinkles to make the cake batter as for the **FUNFETTI LAYER CAKE** (see page 67) and divide between the cupcake cases until just over half-filled. Bake for 15–20 minutes, or until the cakes bounce back when touched or a toothpick inserted into the cupcake comes out clean. Leave to cool on a wire rack.

3 Prepare a batch of **WHIPPED CREAM BUTTERCREAM** (see page 17) using the quantities listed here for the butter, icing sugar, double cream and white chocolate.

4 Put 5 tablespoons each of the buttercream into six bowls. Use a touch of gel food colouring to colour one each pink, orange, yellow, green, blue and purple. Add just a little colouring at a time to achieve pastel shades.

5 Using the multi-tone piping method (see page 24) – with white buttercream being the majority colour and the other colours piped in lines on top – load the buttercreams into a piping bag fitted with your nozzle of choice. Pipe a classic rosette or swirl on top of each cupcake (see page 26).

6 Decorate with sprinkles, sweets and edible glitter.

To make cake jars

Follow the method above to make 12 funfetti cupcakes (undecorated) and the whipped cream buttercream.

You will need 3 cupcakes or 150g (5oz) of cake per jar. When making a cake jar that contains no other fillings apart from the buttercream, pipe a thicker layer of buttercream to compensate.

Alternatively, take this cake jar to the next level by adding a teaspoon of white chocolate spread filling to each layer.

Fill the jars in layers following the cake jar tutorial on page 55.

CHERRY BAKEWELL CAKE

Perfectly potent red sponge... with an almond kick! This showstopper is for Bakewell fans everywhere. It has a beautiful almond aroma and looks particularly majestic when studded with glacé cherries and flaked almonds, and topped with mini Bakewell tarts.

INGREDIENTS

Makes a 20cm (8in), 4-layer cake

600g (5 sticks) unsalted butter

600g (3 cups) caster sugar

10 eggs

2 tbsp almond extract

300g (10oz) glacé cherries

450g (3½ cups) self-raising flour

150g (1¼ cups) almond flour

Red gel food colouring
(we use Sugarflair Red Extra)

Flavoured buttercream

250g (2 sticks) unsalted butter

500g (3½ cups) icing sugar

1 tbsp almond extract

Filling

150g (½ cup) cherry jam

Decoration

500g (4 sticks plus 2 tbsp) unsalted butter

1kg (7 cups) icing sugar

2 tbsp almond extract

15g (4 tsp) whitening powder (optional)

Red gel food colouring
(we use Sugarflair Red Extra)

Gold and red sprinkles, flaked almonds, glacé cherries, Bakewell tarts (store-bought, optional), Cherry Bakewell Cupcakes (see page 73) and edible glitter

SPECIAL EQUIPMENT

Mixer or hand-held electric whisk

4 x 20cm (8in) cake tins, lined

Cake drum, turntable and dowels

Straight-edge and bubble scrapers

1 Preheat the oven to 180°C (160°C fan/350°F/Gas 4).

2 Put the butter and sugar into a mixer bowl and, using the paddle attachment, cream together on a high speed. Alternatively, use a large mixing bowl and a hand-held electric whisk.

3 When the butter and sugar are combined and the butter has changed to a paler colour, turn the mixer speed down to medium. Add the eggs, one by one, until combined, then add the almond extract.

4 Lightly coat the glacé cherries in some of the self-raising flour. This will prevent them from sinking in the batter.

5 Add the almond flour to the creamed mixture and sift in the self-raising flour. Add the coated cherries and a few drops of red extra food colouring to create a marbled effect. Fold it all together using a spatula, or combine in the mixer using a low speed setting. Do not overmix.

6 Divide the batter evenly among the lined tins. Bake in the oven for 30–35 minutes, or until the sponge bounces back when pressed. You can also check by inserting a toothpick into the centre; if it comes out clean, the cake is ready.

7 Allow to cool in the tins for 5–10 minutes, then carefully turn out onto wire racks and leave to cool completely.

Filling and stacking

8 Make a batch of **FLAVOURED BUTTERCREAM** (see page 16), adding the almond extract.

9 Level and stack the cake following the instructions for a cake with filling on pages 34–35, using cherry jam with the buttercream. Dowel the cake, if required. ▶

10 Chill the cake in the fridge for 30 minutes until the buttercream has solidified, then add a crumb coat (see page 39) using the remaining buttercream. Chill the cake for 30 minutes or until you are ready to decorate.

Decoration

11 Make a large batch of **FLAVOURED BUTTERCREAM** using the quantities listed on page 71 for the butter, icing sugar and almond extract. For a whiter buttercream, sift the whitening powder into the bowl and mix in.

12 Take the cake out of the fridge and place onto a turntable. Use a straight-edge scraper to smooth some of the buttercream onto the edges of the cake (see page 40). Chill the cake for 15 minutes. Meanwhile, colour the remaining white buttercream red.

13 Use the fault line technique (see page 44) around the top and bottom of the cake, finishing it with a bubble scraper. Decorate the fault line with sprinkles and flaked almonds.

14 Load a piping bag with the remaining red buttercream and pipe rosettes (see page 26) all over the top of the cake and around the base of the cake board.

15 Use sliced and whole Bakewell tarts, glacé cherries and flaked almonds to decorate the top of the cake – we did this in a crescent moon shape. We also added a couple of **CHERRY BAKEWELL CUPCAKES** (see recipe, opposite) and edible glitter.

16 Chill the cake in the fridge for a couple of hours, or until the day you are cutting the cake.

CHERRY BAKEWELL CUPCAKES & JARS

INGREDIENTS

Makes 12 cupcakes / 4 cake jars

180g (1½ sticks) unsalted butter

180g (¾ cup plus 2 tbsp) caster sugar

3 eggs

130g (1 cup) self-raising flour

50g (⅓ cup plus 1 tbsp) almond flour

50g (1¾oz) glacé cherries

1 tsp almond extract

Red gel food colouring

Flavoured buttercream

200g (1 stick plus 5 tbsp) unsalted butter

400g (3⅓ cups) icing sugar

Almond extract, to taste

Filling

200g (⅔ cup) cherry jam

Decoration

Flaked almonds

12 glacé cherries

SPECIAL EQUIPMENT

Mixer or hand-held electric whisk

12-hole cupcake tin, lined with cases

Piping bag and Rachel #2D or Emily #1E nozzle (or nozzle of choice)

1 Follow steps 1–5 of the **CHERRY BAKEWELL CAKE** (see page 71) to make the cake batter, but using the cupcake quantities listed here for the butter, caster sugar, eggs, self-raising and almond flour, glacé cherries, almond extract and food colouring.

2 Divide the batter between the cupcake cases, filling each one just over halfway.

3 Bake in the oven for 15–20 minutes, or until the cupcakes spring back when pressed. Transfer to a wire rack to cool.

4 While they are baking, prepare the **FLAVOURED BUTTERCREAM** (see page 16), using the quantities listed here and adding almond extract to taste. Fill a piping bag fitted with your nozzle of choice with the buttercream.

5 Core the cupcakes (see page 29) and add a teaspoon of cherry jam or conserve to each. Replace the tops and pipe a classic rosette or swirl of buttercream on top (see page 26).

6 Sprinkle each cupcake with flaked almonds and top each with a glacé cherry.

To make cake jars

If you are not using up leftover sponge or buttercream, follow the method above to make 12 cherry Bakewell cupcakes (undecorated) and the flavoured buttercream.

You will need 3 cupcakes or 150g (5oz) of cake per jar. Allow 50g (3 tbsp) of cherry jam per cake jar.

Fill the jars in layers using the cake jar tutorial on page 55.

CARROT CAKE

Spices, chopped nuts, cream cheese buttercream and, of course, carrots all play a part in this delicious classic. With just enough fruit and vegetables to suggest it may not actually be a cake, this moist and fruity sponge will encourage you to eat your five a day!

INGREDIENTS

Makes a 20cm (8in), 6-layer cake

480g (3⅔ cups) self-raising flour

3½ tsp baking powder

1½ tsp ground mixed spice

1½ tsp ground ginger

¼ tsp salt

360g (1¾ cups) light muscovado sugar

7 eggs

400ml (1⅔ cups) vegetable oil

120g (¾ cup) sultanas (optional)

120g (1 cup) chopped walnuts (optional)

320g (3 cups) grated carrot

Cream cheese buttercream

400g (3 sticks plus 3 tbsp) unsalted butter

1kg (7 cups) icing sugar

300g (10oz) full-fat cream cheese

Lemon juice, to taste

Decoration

Cream cheese buttercream

Fresh fruit

Walnuts (optional)

Icing sugar, for dusting

SPECIAL EQUIPMENT

Mixer or hand-held electric whisk

3 x 20cm (8in) cake tins, lined

28cm (11in) cake drum, turntable and dowels

Piping bag and nozzle of choice

1   Preheat the oven to 180°C (160°C fan/350°F/Gas 4).

2   Sift the flour, baking powder, mixed spice and ginger into the mixer bowl and mix well. Add the salt and muscovado sugar.

3   Set the mixer to low (or use a hand-held electric whisk) and add the eggs, one by one, followed by the vegetable oil. Slowly combine.

4   Using a spatula, gently fold in the sultanas and walnuts, if using, and the carrot.

5   Divide the batter equally between the lined tins. Bake in the preheated oven for 30–35 minutes, or until the sponge bounces back when pressed. You can also check by inserting a sharp knife into the centre. If it comes out clean, the cake is ready.

6   Allow to cool in the tins for 5–10 minutes, then carefully turn out onto wire racks and leave to cool completely.

Filling and stacking

7   Make a batch of **CREAM CHEESE BUTTERCREAM** using the quantities listed here (see page 17 for method).

8   Refer to the information on levelling and torting cakes on page 34 to cut the three cakes in half to create six layers. Stack the cake following the naked cakes technique (see page 36) using the cream cheese buttercream. This cake has no further fillings.

9   Dowel the cake using the method on page 35.

10 Chill the cake in the fridge for 30 minutes until the buttercream has solidified and the cake is sturdy. ▶

Decoration

11 Pipe some cream cheese buttercream on top of the cake and
around the bottom, before decorating with fresh fruit and
walnuts, if using. We have used strawberries, raspberries,
blueberries, blackberries and walnuts.

12 Sift a small amount of icing sugar over the cake before serving.
This cake is best enjoyed fresh.

TOP TIPS

★ Add a teaspoon of ground cinnamon to the cake batter
to give this carrot cake a wintery kick.

★ As the naked cake is not covered with buttercream,
we suggest baking and decorating it a maximum of 24 hours
before it is due to be cut to prevent the sponge from drying out.

CARROT CUPCAKES & JARS

INGREDIENTS

Makes 12 cupcakes / 4 cake jars

185g (1½ cups) self-raising flour

1 tsp baking powder

1 heaped tsp mixed spice

1 heaped tsp ground ginger

Pinch of salt

140g (⅔ cup) light muscovado sugar

2 eggs

150ml (⅔ cup) vegetable oil

50g (⅓ cup) sultanas (optional)

50g (scant ½ cup) chopped walnuts (optional)

Cream cheese buttercream

150g (1 stick plus 2 tbsp) unsalted butter

300g (2 cups plus 2 tbsp) icing sugar, plus extra if needed

100g (3½oz) full-fat cream cheese

A dash of lemon juice

Decoration

Fresh fruit and walnuts (optional)

SPECIAL EQUIPMENT

Mixer or hand-held electric whisk

12-hole cupcake tin, lined with cases

Piping bag and Kim #1C nozzle (or nozzle of choice)

1 Using the cupcake quantities listed here, follow steps 1–4 of the **CARROT CAKE** (see page 77) to make the cake batter.

2 Divide the mixture between the cupcake cases, filling each one by about two-thirds. Bake in the preheated oven for 18–20 minutes, or until the cupcakes spring back when pressed. Allow to cool on a wire rack.

3 While the cupcakes are baking, prepare the **CREAM CHEESE BUTTERCREAM** using the quantities listed here (see page 17 for method).

4 Once the cupcakes have cooled, load a piping bag with your chosen nozzle and the buttercream. Pipe on the cupcakes in your chosen technique – we like a classic swirl for these (see pages 26–29). Decorate the cupcakes with fresh fruit and walnuts, if you like.

To make cake jars

Follow the method above to make 12 carrot cupcakes (undecorated) and the cream cheese buttercream.

You will need 3 cupcakes or 150g (5oz) of cake per jar.

We find that the flavours of the carrot cake sponge and cream cheese buttercream shine without needing any other fillings – when making a cake jar that contains no other fillings, pipe a slightly thicker layer of buttercream to compensate.

Fill the jars in layers using the cake jar tutorial on page 55.

INGREDIENTS

Makes a 20cm (8in), 4-layer cake

600g (5 sticks) unsalted butter

600g (3 cups) caster sugar

10 eggs

600g (4⅔ cups) self-raising flour

Pink, blue and purple gel food colouring

Filling

200g (7oz) Marshmallow Fluff Filling (see page 23) or white chocolate spread

Flavoured buttercream

350g (3 sticks) unsalted butter

700g (5 cups) icing sugar

Candy floss extract, to taste
(we use Foodie Flavours)

5–10g (about ¼oz) whitening powder

Pink, blue and purple gel food colouring

Decoration

500g (4 sticks plus 2 tbsp) unsalted butter

1kg (7 cups) icing sugar

15g (4 tsp) whitening powder

Candy floss extract, to taste

Pink, blue and purple gel food colouring

Candy Floss Macarons (see page 223)

Sprinkles, candy floss and edible glitter

SPECIAL EQUIPMENT

Mixer or hand-held electric whisk

4 x 20cm (8in) cake tins, lined

Cake drum, turntable and dowels (optional)

Straight-edge and bubble scrapers

Piping bags and Erin #1M nozzle (or nozzle of choice)

CANDY FLOSS CAKE

Cut into this pastel buttercream cake with candy-coloured layers sandwiched together with home-made marshmallow fluff. Our candy floss cake recipe looks just as good in cupcake and jar form.

1 Follow steps 1–4 of the **CLASSIC VICTORIA SPONGE** recipe (see page 59) to make the cake batter.

2 Divide the batter evenly among three bowls and colour them pale pink, blue and purple. The more colouring you add, the darker the colour, so start with a little at a time and mix well.

3 Using a different spoon for each, add a quarter of each colour batter into all four lined cake tins – make sure there is the same amount of batter in each. Use an angled spatula or knife to make lines and swirls of colour in the batter, mixing them slightly to create a tie dye or marbled effect.

4 Bake in the preheated oven for 30–35 minutes, or until the sponge bounces back when pressed. If a toothpick inserted into the centre comes out clean, the cake is ready. Let the sponges cool for 5–10 minutes in the tins, then carefully turn out onto wire racks and leave until completely cool.

Filling and stacking

5 Make the **FLAVOURED BUTTERCREAM** (see page 16 for method), using the quantities listed here for the butter and icing sugar; add 3–8 drops of candy floss extract, to taste. Add the whitening powder into the buttercream and mix. Divide the buttercream among three bowls and colour them pink, blue and purple.

6 Level and stack the cake following the instructions for a cake with filling on pages 34–35. Follow the multi-tone piping technique (see page 24) using the pink, blue and purple buttercream and assemble using marshmallow fluff or white chocolate spread as the filling. Dowel the cake, if required (see page 35). Chill the cake for 30 minutes.

7 Crumb coat the cake with the excess buttercream (see page 39) and chill for a further 30 minutes before decorating. ▶

Decoration

8 Make a large batch of **FLAVOURED BUTTERCREAM** using the quantities listed on page 81 for the butter, icing sugar, whitening powder, and 8–12 drops of candy floss extract, to taste. Divide the buttercream into four separate bowls and colour them pink, blue, and purple, and keep one white.

9 Fill a separate piping bag with each colour and snip the end off each one. Follow the watercolour technique on page 47 to apply the buttercream to the crumb-coated cake, finishing with a bubble scraper.

10 Once smooth, chill the cake for at least 1 hour, then trim the top of the cake with a knife until level.

11 Follow the multi-tone piping technique (see page 24) to fill a piping bag fitted with your nozzle of choice, using the excess pink, blue and purple buttercream in the piping bag. Using even pressure, pipe medium-sized whips around the top edge of the cake and smaller ones in the middle and around the base.

12 Decorate with candy floss macarons, sprinkles, candy floss and edible glitter!

CANDY FLOSS CUPCAKES & JARS

INGREDIENTS

Makes 12 cupcakes / 4 cake jars

120g (1 stick) unsalted butter

120g (generous ½ cup) caster sugar

2 eggs

120g (scant 1 cup) self-raising flour

Blue, pink and purple gel food colouring

Filling

200g (7oz) Marshmallow Fluff Filling (see page 23) or white chocolate spread

Flavoured buttercream

125g (1 stick) unsalted butter

250g (1¾ cups) icing sugar

Candy Floss extract, to taste *(we use Foodie Flavours)*

5g (⅙oz) whitening powder

Pink, blue and purple gel food colouring

Decoration

Sprinkles, candy floss and edible glitter

SPECIAL EQUIPMENT

Mixer or hand-held electric whisk

12-hole cupcake tin, lined with cases

Piping bag and nozzle of choice

---

1   Follow the method in steps 1–4 of the **CLASSIC VICTORIA SPONGE** recipe (see page 59), using the quantities listed here to make the cupcake batter.

2   Divide the batter among three bowls and colour them pale pink, blue and purple. The more colouring you add, the darker the colour, so add a little at a time and make sure it is fully incorporated.

3   Using a teaspoon, divide the batters between the cupcake cases, filling each just over half-way and making sure there is a little of each colour in every case. Swirl the colours together using a cocktail stick.

4   Bake for 20 minutes, or until the cupcakes bounce back when pressed. Allow to cool on a wire rack.

5   Core the cupcakes (see page 29) and fill each with a teaspoon of marshmallow fluff or white chocolate spread. Replace the tops.

6   Make a batch of **FLAVOURED BUTTERCREAM** (see page 16 for method) using the quantities listed here, and adding 3-6 drops of candy floss extract to taste. Add the whitening powder and mix in well. Divide the buttercream among four bowls and colour them pink, blue and purple, leaving one white.

7   Follow the multi-tone piping method (see page 24) to load the four colours of buttercream into a piping bag fitted with your nozzle of choice. With an even pressure, pipe a classic rosette (see page 26) on top of each cupcake and tail off. Decorate with sprinkles, candy floss and edible glitter.

To make cake jars

Follow the method above to make 12 candy floss cupcakes (undecorated) and the flavoured buttercream.

You will need 3 cupcakes or 150g (5oz) of cake per jar. Allow 50g (3 tbsp) of marshmallow fluff or white chocolate spread per jar.

Fill the jars in layers using the cake jar tutorial on page 55.

RED VELVET CAKE

Red velvet cake is a delicious blend of vanilla with a hint of chocolate. The buttermilk in this cake is essential to keep the sponge light. Red food colouring is used to give the sponge a vibrant colour, which contrasts with the cream cheese buttercream, making for a delightful taste and a striking look.

INGREDIENTS

Makes a 20cm (8in), 4-layer cake

300g (2½ sticks) unsalted butter

520g (2⅓ cups) caster sugar

6 eggs

2 tsp apple cider vinegar

1½ tsp vanilla extract

360ml (1½ cups) buttermilk

1 tsp red gel food colouring

440g (3⅓ cups) self-raising flour

80g (¾ cup) cocoa powder

1 tsp bicarbonate of soda

Cream cheese buttercream

325g (2 sticks plus 5 tbsp) unsalted butter

900g (7½ cups) icing sugar

220g (8oz) full-fat cream cheese

A dash of lemon juice (optional)

10g (1 tbsp) whitening powder or white food colouring (optional)

Decoration

Freeze-dried raspberry pieces

75g (5 tbsp) unsalted butter

150g (1⅓ cups) icing sugar

A dash of vanilla extract

Green and red gel food colouring

SPECIAL EQUIPMENT

Mixer or hand-held electric whisk

4 x 20cm (8in) cake tins, lined

28cm (11in) cake drum, turntable and dowels (optional)

Piping bags and Erin #1M, Lauren #125 and Hannah #70 nozzles (or nozzles of choice)

Flower nail

1 Preheat the oven to 180°C (160°C fan/350°F/Gas 4).

2 Cream the butter and sugar together in a mixer with the paddle attachment on a high speed. Scrape down the sides of the bowl and mix again on a medium speed, adding in the eggs, one by one, and then the vinegar and vanilla extract. Alternatively, use a mixing bowl and hand-held electric whisk.

3 Mix together the buttermilk and red food colouring until the buttermilk turns red.

4 Sift the flour, cocoa powder and bicarbonate of soda into a separate bowl and mix together until combined.

5 Add around one-third of the red buttermilk to the butter mixture and beat to combine, then add one-third of the dry mixture and beat again. Repeat until everything has been added, mixing as you go on a medium speed setting. The buttermilk may look curdled throughout this process but the dry ingredients will bring it all together.

6 Divide the batter equally among the lined tins. Bake in the preheated oven for 30–35 minutes, or until the sponge bounces back when pressed. You can also check by inserting a sharp knife into the centre; if it comes out clean, the cake is ready.

7 Allow to cool in the tins for 5–10 minutes, then carefully turn out onto wire racks and leave to cool completely.

Filling and stacking

8 Make a batch of **CREAM CHEESE BUTTERCREAM** (see page 17 for method) using the quantities listed here – whip the butter for at least 10 minutes to make it turn as white as possible. Add the whitening powder or white food colouring, if using. ▶

9   Level and stack the cake following the instructions on pages 34–35 for a cake without filling; red velvet cake only tends to have cream cheese buttercream inside. Use the cake off-cuts to make crumbs for the decoration of the cake.

10   Dowel the cake using the method on page 35 (optional).

11   Chill the cake in the fridge for 30 minutes until the buttercream has solidified and the cake is sturdy.

Decoration

12   Use the leftover cream cheese buttercream from filling the cake, and follow the crumb coating technique (see tip for semi-naked finish, page 39). Make sure to take care and time during this step as the semi-naked finished is the final look.

13   Load a piping bag with your nozzle of choice. Pipe small classic rosettes (see page 26) around the bottom of the cake, covering the cake drum. Use the saved red velvet cake crumb and scatter loosely around the bottom and over the top of the cake. We have also sprinkled over freeze-dried raspberry pieces.

14   Prepare a small batch of **VANILLA BUTTERCREAM** using the quantities listed on page 85 for the butter, icing sugar and vanilla extract (see page 16 for method). Colour a small amount green for the leaves, and the rest red (mix in a sprinkle of cocoa powder if you would like a deeper red).

15   Pipe the roses (see page 29 for technique) using a flower nail. Chill each rose in the fridge or freezer until it can be handled. Repeat until you have enough roses; we made 12 for this cake.

16   Once chilled, arrange the roses on the top of the cake and around the base, then pipe the green buttercream on as leaves. We have also decorated the cake with some white chocolate brush strokes (see page 32).

17   Chill in the fridge for a couple of hours, or until the day you are cutting the cake.

TOP TIP

★ The red velvet's colour was not originally enhanced with food colouring but you can now find reliable products to help you achieve a true red. You often need quite a lot of red food colouring to reach the desired pigment – we recommend using a gel as liquid food colouring will often disperse while cooking, compromising the colour of the sponge. Some red food colourings contain the E number E120 which may not be suitable for vegans and vegetarians. We use Sugarflair Red Extra in this recipe.

RED VELVET CUPCAKES & JARS

INGREDIENTS

Makes 12 cupcakes / 4 cake jars

100g (6½ tbsp) unsalted butter

175g (¾ cup plus 2 tbsp) caster sugar

2 eggs

15g (1½ tbsp) cocoa powder

150g (1 cup plus 3 tbsp) self-raising flour

125ml (½ cup) buttermilk

½ tsp bicarbonate of soda

½ tsp apple cider vinegar

¼ tsp red gel food colouring

½ tsp vanilla extract

Cream cheese buttercream

150g (1 stick plus 2 tbsp) unsalted butter

300g (2 cups plus 2 tbsp) icing sugar

100g (3½oz) full-fat cream cheese

A dash of lemon juice

Decoration

Red velvet cake crumbs

SPECIAL EQUIPMENT

Mixer or hand-held electric whisk

12-hole cupcake tin, lined with cases

Piping bag and Isabel #9FT nozzle (or nozzle of choice)

1 Use the quantities listed here to make the cupcake batter, following steps 1–5 of the method for the **RED VELVET CAKE** (see page 85).

2 Divide the batter between the cupcake cases until each one is just over half-filled and bake for 18–20 minutes, or until the cupcakes bounce back when touched or a toothpick inserted into the cupcake comes out clean. Leave to cool on a wire rack.

3 While the cupcakes are in the oven, prepare the **CREAM CHEESE BUTTERCREAM** (see page 17) using the quantities listed here.

4 Once cooled, slice a small amount of cake off the top of a couple of cupcakes and crumble into a small bowl. Set aside for decoration.

5 Load the piping bag with your chosen nozzle and the cream cheese buttercream and pipe the cupcakes using any technique you like (see pages 26–29). Sprinkle the red cake crumbs over the top to decorate.

To make cake jars

Follow the method above to make 12 red velvet cupcakes (undecorated) and the cream cheese buttercream.

You will need 3 cupcakes or 150g (5oz) of cake per jar.

We find that the flavours of the red velvet sponge and cream cheese buttercream are delicious without needing any other fillings – when making a cake jar that contains no other fillings, pipe a slightly thicker layer of buttercream to compensate.

Fill the jars in layers using the cake jar tutorial on page 55.

Makes a 20cm (8in), 4-layer cake

- 300ml (1¼ cups) vegetable oil
- 6 eggs
- 360g (1½ cups) smooth peanut butter
- 360ml (1½ cups) milk
- 300ml (1¼ cups) soured cream
- 440g (2¼ cups packed) light soft brown sugar
- 440g (3⅓ cups) self-raising flour
- 1 tsp salt
- 2 tsp baking powder
- 300g (10oz) peanut butter chips or chocolate chips (or a mixture)

Chocolate whipped cream buttercream

- 250g (2 sticks) unsalted butter
- 450g (3¼ cups) icing sugar
- 100ml (6½ tbsp) double cream
- 50g (½ cup) cocoa powder
- 250g (9oz) milk or dark chocolate
- Pinch of salt

Decoration

- 1 batch of Peanut Butter Cups (see page 201)
- 100g (3½oz) milk chocolate
- 500g (4 sticks plus 2 tbsp) unsalted butter
- 1kg (7 cups) icing sugar
- 200g (¾ cup plus 2 tbsp) smooth peanut butter
- 100g (3½oz) chocolate spread
- Bronze sprinkles, peanut butter chocolates and chocolate-coated peanuts
- 5g (1 tsp) cocoa powder

SPECIAL EQUIPMENT

- Mixer or hand-held electric whisk
- 4 x 20cm (8in) cake tins, lined
- 28cm (11in) cake drum, turntable and dowels (optional)
- Piping bag and nozzle of choice

PEANUT BUTTER CAKE

This American-style sponge is light and airy when baked as a cupcake and dense and full of flavour as a layer cake. Teamed with chocolate whipped cream buttercream and peanut butter chocolate chips, this one is the ultimate indulgence for peanut butter lovers everywhere.

1   Preheat the oven to 180°C (160°C fan/350°F/Gas 4).

2   Combine the wet ingredients together in a bowl: the vegetable oil, eggs, peanut butter, milk and soured cream. Add in the brown sugar and mix until combined.

3   Sift the flour, salt and baking powder into the bowl and fold in with a spatula or mix on a very slow speed. The mixture should be a thick liquid. Add in the peanut butter chips or chocolate chips (or a combination of the two!) and mix.

4   Divide the batter evenly between the lined tins. Bake in the preheated oven for 30–35 minutes, or until the sponge bounces back when pressed. You can also check by inserting a sharp knife into the centre; if it comes out clean, the cake is ready.

5   Allow the sponges to cool in the tins for 5–10 minutes, then carefully turn out onto wire racks and leave to cool completely.

Filling and stacking

6   Make a batch of **CHOCOLATE WHIPPED CREAM BUTTERCREAM** (see page 17 for method).

7   Level and stack the cake following the instructions on pages 34–35, for a cake without filling.

8   Dowel the cake using the method on page 35 (optional).

9   Chill the cake in the fridge for 30 minutes until the buttercream has solidified. Crumb coat the cake (see page 39) with the remaining buttercream. Chill for a further 30 minutes, or until you are ready to decorate. ▶

Decoration

10 Make the **PEANUT BUTTER CUPS** (see page 201). Leave to set.

11 Use the milk chocolate to make a tempered chocolate sail (see page 32). Leave to set.

12 Make a batch of **FLAVOURED BUTTERCREAM**, using the quantities listed on page 89 for the butter, icing sugar and the smooth peanut butter (see page 16 for method). You may want to melt the peanut butter for a few seconds in the microwave first to make it easier to mix in.

13 Apply and smooth the buttercream (see pages 39–40). Save the excess buttercream to decorate the top of the cake.

14 Melt the chocolate spread to create a drip (see page 50). Chill the cake for 15 minutes, or until the drip has set. Add bronze sprinkles whilst the drip is still tacky.

15 Mix the cocoa powder into the remaining buttercream and load it into a piping bag fitted with your nozzle of choice. Pipe stars (see page 27) all over the top of the cake and around the base.

16 To decorate, arrange the peanut butter cups, chocolate sail, peanut butter chocolates and chocolate-coated peanuts on the cake.

17 Chill the cake in the fridge for 30 minutes or until the day you are cutting it.

TOP TIP ★

As peanut butter is so drying, this recipe calls for a few changes to what is usually used in cake batter. Replacing the butter with oil and soured cream enables all the moisture needed to retain the flavour of peanut butter, whilst maintaining a lovely texture.

PEANUT BUTTER CUPCAKES & JARS

INGREDIENTS

Makes 12 cupcakes / 4 cake jars

- 100ml (6½ tbsp) vegetable oil
- 2 eggs
- 120g (½ cup) peanut butter
- 120ml (½ cup) milk
- 65g (¼ cup) soured cream
- 150g (¾ cup packed) light soft brown sugar
- 150g (1 cup plus 3 tbsp) self-raising flour
- Pinch of salt
- ½ tsp baking powder
- 100g (3½oz) peanut butter chips or chocolate chips

Chocolate whipped cream buttercream

- 125g (4oz) milk or dark chocolate
- 125g (1 stick) unsalted butter
- 225g (2 cups) icing sugar
- 25g (¼ cup) cocoa powder
- 50ml (3½ tbsp) double cream

Decoration

- Dark chocolate ganache, for drizzling (see page 19)
- Peanut butter chips, 12 Maltesers and edible gold lustre dust

SPECIAL EQUIPMENT

- Mixer or hand-held electric whisk
- 12-hole cupcake tin, lined with cases
- Piping bag and nozzle of choice

1 Use the quantities listed here to make the cupcake batter, following steps 1–3 for the **PEANUT BUTTER CAKE** (see page 89).

2 Divide the batter between the cupcake cases until each one is three-quarters filled and bake for 20–22 minutes, or until the cupcakes bounce back when touched or a toothpick inserted into the cupcake comes out clean. Leave to cool on a wire rack.

3 Prepare a batch of **CHOCOLATE WHIPPED CREAM BUTTERCREAM** using the quantities listed here (see page 17 for method). Load into a piping bag fitted with your preferred nozzle, and pipe a classic swirl on top of each cupcake (see page 26).

4 Drizzle with dark chocolate ganache and top with more peanut butter chips. Roll the Maltesers in gold lustre dust, and top the cakes with them to finish!

To make cake jars

Follow the method above to make 12 peanut butter cupcakes (undecorated) and the chocolate whipped cream buttercream.

You will need 3 cupcakes or 150g (5oz) of cake per jar.

We find that the flavours of the peanut butter sponge and chocolate whipped cream buttercream are a great combination without any other fillings – when making a cake jar that contains no other fillings, pipe a slightly thicker layer of buttercream to compensate.

Fill the jars in layers using the cake jar tutorial on page 55.

STICKY TOFFEE PUDDING CAKE

Our delicious sticky toffee pudding cake – or STP, as we call it at Finch Bakery – is our absolute favourite sponge flavour. We often wonder why anyone would order anything else when picking a restaurant dessert... or a Finch Bakery birthday cake! Whether you're making cupcakes, a celebration cake or cake jars, our much requested recipe is the perfect pudding for all year round!

INGREDIENTS

Makes a 20cm (8in), 4-layer cake

480g (4 sticks) unsalted butter

600g (3 cups) light muscovado sugar

240g (1 cup) black treacle

240g (1 cup) golden syrup

5 eggs

480ml (2 cups) milk

600g (4⅔ cups) plain flour

12g (1 tbsp) bicarbonate of soda

Flavoured buttercream

250g (2 sticks) unsalted butter

500g (3½ cups) icing sugar

50g (3 tbsp) black treacle

Filling

180g (½ cup) caramel
(see page 21 or use store-bought caramel sauce)

Decoration

Chocolate Caramel Brownies
(see page 152)

500g (4 sticks plus 2 tbsp) unsalted butter

1kg (7 cups) icing sugar

100g (6 tbsp) black treacle

1 or 2 squares of white chocolate

Toffee popcorn, fudge pieces and caramel chocolates

SPECIAL EQUIPMENT

Mixer or hand-held electric whisk

4 x 20cm (8in) cake tins, lined

28cm (11in) cake drum, turntable, 15–17.5cm (6–7in) thin cake board and dowels

Piping bags and Erin #1M nozzle (or nozzle of choice)

1   Preheat the oven to 180°C (160°C fan/350°F/Gas 4).

2   Melt the butter, sugar, black treacle and syrup together in a pan on the hob over a low heat until melted. Stir until all of the sugar has dissolved and all of the ingredients have combined. Alternatively, microwave at full power, checking and stirring the mix at 20-second intervals until liquified and combined.

3   Pour into a mixer bowl (or use a mixing bowl and hand-held electric whisk) and add the eggs and milk; combine on a low setting. Sift the flour and bicarbonate of soda into the wet mixture and combine again. Eventually it will turn into a dark brown batter, and lumps are likely to be visible.

4   Pour the liquid through a sieve into another clean bowl to remove any lumps. The batter will be very thin.

5   Divide the batter equally among the lined tins. Bake in the preheated oven for 30–35 minutes, or until the sponge bounces back when pressed (however, please note this sponge is sticky compared to normal sponge). You can also check by inserting a knife tip into the centre; if it comes out clean, the cake is ready.

6   Allow to cool in the tins for 5–10 minutes, then carefully turn out onto wire racks and leave to cool completely.

Filling and stacking

7   Make a batch of **FLAVOURED BUTTERCREAM**, adding in the treacle (see page 16 for method). ▶

8 Level and stack the cake following the instructions on pages 34–35 for a cake with filling, using the caramel filling (see page 21, but hold the salt!). Save the excess caramel for the drip.

9 Dowel the cake using the method on page 35. Chill the cake for 30 minutes until the buttercream has solidified.

Decoration

10 Prepare a batch of **CHOCOLATE CARAMEL BROWNIES** (see page 152) and leave to cool completely before cutting. These are to decorate the top of the cake.

11 Make a large batch of **FLAVOURED BUTTERCREAM** using the quantities listed on page 95 for the butter, icing sugar and treacle (see page 16 for method). Apply and smooth the buttercream (see pages 39–40). Save any excess for later.

12 Apply a little buttercream on top of the dowels to secure a thin cake board on top of the cake. This is to support the decoration.

13 Gently heat the remaining caramel and add a cube or two of white chocolate, stirring until melted together. Leave to cool for a few minutes and use the back of a spoon to create a caramel drip (see page 50). Chill until the drip has set. Meanwhile, cut the caramel brownies into cubes.

14 Load a piping bag with your nozzle of choice and the remaining buttercream. Pipe small rosettes (see page 26) around the base of the cake and around the top, to cover the lip of the cake and the thin cake board. Pipe small open stars (see page 27) all over the cake board, completely covering it with buttercream.

15 Position the larger pieces of brownie inside the rosettes in a circle. Pipe some more small open stars on top of the brownie, then create another circle of brownies, slightly smaller than the first – around 1cm (½in) in. Continue in this way, sticking them together with buttercream, to create a brownie pyramid.

16 Use buttercream to fill in the gaps and stick on toffee popcorn and fudge pieces. Decorate around the base with brownies, popcorn, fudge and caramel chocolates. Chill until ready to cut.

TOP TIPS

★ If you don't have light muscovado sugar, you can replace this with a mixture of light and dark soft brown sugar. We would use half and half for this recipe.

★ The strength of the treacle buttercream is to your taste – add more or less than the suggested amount.

STICKY TOFFEE CUPCAKES & JARS

INGREDIENTS

Makes 12 cupcakes / 4 cake jars

125g (1 stick) unsalted butter

150g (¾ cup) light muscovado sugar

65g (⅓ cup) black treacle

65g (⅓ cup) golden syrup

125ml (½ cup) milk

150g (1 cup plus 2 tbsp) plain flour

1 egg

¾ tsp bicarbonate of soda

Filling

4 tbsp caramel (see page 21 or use store-bought caramel sauce)

Flavoured buttercream

170g (1 stick plus 3 tbsp) unsalted butter

350g (2⅓ cups) icing sugar

35g (2 tbsp) black treacle, or to taste

Decoration

Extra caramel, to drizzle,

Fudge pieces, chocolates and sprinkles

SPECIAL EQUIPMENT

Mixer or hand-held electric whisk

12-hole cupcake tin, lined with cases

Piping bag and nozzle of choice

1   Use the quantities listed here to make the cupcake batter, following steps 1–4 of the **STICKY TOFFEE PUDDING CAKE** (see page 95).

2   Pour the liquid batter into a jug (this will help with control) and then into the cupcake cases until just over half-filled. Bake for 20–25 minutes, or until the cupcakes bounce back when touched or a toothpick inserted into the cupcake comes out clean.

3   Leave the cupcakes to cool in the tin for 5 minutes before transferring them to a wire rack to cool completely.

4   Core the cupcakes (see page 29) and fill with each with 1 teaspoon of caramel sauce.

5   Make the **FLAVOURED BUTTERCREAM** with the quantities listed here for the butter and icing sugar (see page 16 for method). Add the treacle a little at a time, to taste.

6   Pipe the buttercream onto the top of the cupcakes, from the outside in, using even pressure to create a classic swirl (see page 26).

7   You can enjoy these plain or decorate with an extra drizzle of caramel over the top and some fudge pieces and chocolates.

To make cake jars

Follow the method above to make 12 sticky toffee cupcakes (undecorated) and the flavoured buttercream.

You will need 3 cupcakes or 150g (5oz) of cake per jar.

Allow 50g (about 3 tbsp) of caramel per cake jar. Caramel should not be made in small portions, so we recommend to making a full batch of caramel (see page 20) and saving any left over for later.

Fill the jars in layers using the cake jar tutorial on page 55.

Makes a 20cm (8in), 4-layer cake

480g (4 sticks) unsalted butter

400g (2 cups packed) light soft brown sugar

10 eggs

300g (1¼ cups) Lotus Biscoff spread

300ml (1¼ cups) soured cream

1 tsp vanilla extract

250g (9oz) Lotus Biscoff biscuits

480g (3⅔ cups) self-raising flour

1 tsp baking powder

Flavoured buttercream

250g (2 sticks) unsalted butter

500g (3½ cups) icing sugar

200g (¾ cup plus 1 tbsp) Lotus Biscoff spread

A dash of vanilla extract

Ganache balls

300g (10oz) white chocolate

150g (⅔ cup) double cream

3 tablespoons Lotus Biscoff spread

150g (5oz) packet Lotus Biscoff Sandwich Original Cream biscuits

Decoration

500g (4 sticks plus 2 tbsp) unsalted butter

1kg (7 cups) icing sugar

350g (1½ cups) Lotus Biscoff spread

80g (3oz) Lotus Biscoff biscuits, crushed, plus 5 whole

Caramel chocolates

SPECIAL EQUIPMENT

Mixer or hand-held electric whisk

4 x 20cm (8in) cake tins, lined

Cake drum, turntable and dowels (optional)

Straight-edge scraper

Scallop scraper

Piping bags and nozzles of choice

LOTUS BISCOFF CAKE

Biscuit taste, cake texture! Lotus Biscoff is one of our top flavours and a staple ingredient in our bakery. This recipe is sure to be a winner for whoever you're serving it up to. If the crushed biscuits in the sponge aren't enough, this cake also contains Lotus Biscoff spread and buttercream!

1   Preheat the oven to 180°C (160°C fan/350°F/Gas 4).

2   Put the butter and light soft brown sugar into the bowl of a mixer (or use a mixing bowl and a hand-held electric whisk). Using the paddle attachment, cream together on a high speed until combined and pale in colour. Turn the mixer speed down to medium. Add the eggs, one by one, until combined.

3   Soften the Lotus Biscoff spread in a bowl in the microwave at full power, blasting it for 10–20 seconds. Add it to the butter and sugar mixture, along with the soured cream and vanilla. Mix.

4   Use a rolling pin to crush the Lotus Biscoff biscuits in a bowl; there should be mainly crumb with some larger pieces left.

5   Sift the flour and baking powder into the bowl and fold in with a spatula or mix on a very slow speed. Add the crushed biscuits and mix until combined.

6   Divide the batter equally between the lined tins and bake in the preheated oven for 30–35 minutes, or until the sponge bounces back when pressed. You can also check by inserting a sharp knife into the centre; if it comes out clean, the cake is ready.

7   Allow to cool in the tins for 5–10 minutes, then carefully turn out onto wire racks and leave to cool completely.

Filling and stacking

8   Make a batch of Lotus Biscoff **FLAVOURED BUTTERCREAM** (see page 16 for method) – soften the Lotus Biscoff spread in a bowl for a few seconds in the microwave at full power before mixing it into the buttercream. ▶

9 Level and stack the cake following the instructions on pages 34–35, using more softened lotus spread as the filling. Dowel the cake using the method on page 35 (optional).

10 Chill the cake in the fridge for 30 minutes until the buttercream has solidified. Crumb coat the cake (see page 39) with the remaining buttercream. Chill for a further 30 minutes, or until you are ready to decorate.

Decoration

11 Make a batch of **CHOCOLATE GANACHE BALLS** (see page 202), using the quantities given here, adding 1 tablespoon of Lotus spread to the melted white chocolate and 2 tablespoons to the ganache while whipping. Leave to set.

12 Make a batch of **FLAVOURED BUTTERCREAM** (see page 16) using the quantities listed on page 99 for the butter and icing sugar, and add 300g (1¼ cups) of the Lotus Biscoff spread, softened in the microwave at full power first.

13 Apply and smooth the buttercream, finishing using a scallop scraper (see pages 39–40). Save the excess buttercream to decorate the top of the cake.

14 With a gloved hand, lightly pat some of the crushed Lotus biscuits onto the lower half of the cake until moderately covered.

15 Melt the remaining 50g (¼ cup) Lotus Biscoff spread in a bowl in the microwave at full power. Use the back of a spoon to create a drip (see page 50). Chill the cake in the fridge for 15 minutes, or until the drip becomes tacky.

16 Load a piping bag with the rest of the buttercream and pipe small swirls all over the top of the cake and small rosettes around the bottom (see page 26).

17 Decorate with the ganache balls, caramel chocolates and the 5 whole Lotus biscuits. Sprinkle any excess crumbs over the top. Chill for 30 minutes or until the day of cutting.

TOP TIPS

★ Using light soft brown sugar really brings out the caramel colour and flavour required to complement the biscuit in this recipe.

★ One of our favourite flavours to team Biscoff with is salted caramel – swap the Lotus spread filling with our Salted Caramel recipe (see page 21) for another option.

★ You can also swap Lotus Biscoff crushed biscuits for Lotus Biscoff Crumb – pre-crushed!

LOTUS BISCOFF CUPCAKES & JARS

INGREDIENTS

Makes 12 cupcakes / 4 cake jars

120g (1 stick) unsalted butter or margarine, softened

100g (½ cup packed) light soft brown sugar

3 eggs

75g (⅓ cup) Lotus Biscoff spread

75ml (⅓ cup) soured cream

A few drops of vanilla extract

6 Lotus Biscoff biscuits

120g (scant 1 cup) self-raising flour

½ tsp baking powder

Flavoured buttercream

125g (1 stick) unsalted butter

250g (1¾ cups) icing sugar

75g (⅓ cup) Lotus Biscoff spread

Filling

200g (7oz) Lotus Biscoff spread

Decoration

Lotus Biscoff spread, to drizzle

Lotus Biscoff biscuits/crumbs

SPECIAL EQUIPMENT

Mixer or hand-held electric whisk

12-hole cupcake tin, lined with cases

Piping bag and Steph #1G nozzle (or nozzle of choice)

1   Use the quantities listed here to make the cupcakes, following the method in steps 1–5 of the **LOTUS BISCOFF CAKE** recipe (see page 99).

2   Divide the batter between the cupcake cases until each one is just over half-filled and bake for 20–22 minutes, or until the cupcakes bounce back when touched (or a toothpick inserted into the cupcake comes out clean). Leave to cool on a wire rack.

3   Use the quantities given here to prepare a batch of Lotus Biscoff **FLAVOURED BUTTERCREAM** (see page 16). Soften the Lotus Biscoff spread in the microwave at full power and combine with the buttercream until smooth and pale brown.

4   Once the cupcakes are cool, core them using a teaspoon (see page 29). Fill the middle of each with a teaspoon of softened Biscoff spread (melt it in the microwave at full power) and replace the tops.

5   Load the piping bag with the Biscoff buttercream and pipe a classic swirl with a whip (see page 26) on each cupcake. Decorate with a drizzle of melted Biscoff spread, whole Lotus biscuits and a sprinkle of crumbled Lotus biscuit or crumbs.

To make cake jars

Follow the method above to make 12 Lotus Biscoff cupcakes (undecorated) and the Lotus Biscoff flavoured buttercream.

You will need 3 cupcakes or 150g (5oz) of cake per jar. Allow 50g (about 3 tbsp) of melted Lotus Biscoff spread per cake jar.

Fill the jars in layers using the cake jar tutorial on page 55.

CREME EGG CAKE

This is the ultimate recipe for using up your springtime stash of Creme Eggs to decorate this indulgent Easter showstopper or for satisfying your Creme Egg cravings all year round!

INGREDIENTS

Makes a 20cm (8in), 4-layer cake

600g (5 sticks) unsalted butter

600g (3 cups) caster sugar

10 eggs

600g (4⅔ cups) self-raising flour

Orange gel food colouring

Creme Egg filling

35g (3 tbsp) caster sugar

35ml (2 tbsp plus 1 tsp) water

400g (14oz) white fondant

A few drops of vanilla extract

30ml (2 tbsp) glycerine

Orange gel food colouring

Chocolate buttercream

375g (3 sticks) unsalted butter

675g (5½ cups) icing sugar

100g (1 cup) cocoa powder

Decoration

500g (4 sticks plus 2 tbsp) unsalted butter

1kg (7 cups) icing sugar

Vanilla extract, to taste

15g (4 tsp) whitening powder (optional)

Orange gel food colouring

Chocolates, gold leaf, Cadbury's Creme Eggs, sprinkles and edible glitter

SPECIAL EQUIPMENT

Mixer or hand-held electric whisk

Piping bags and Erin #1M nozzle (or nozzle of choice)

4 x 20cm (8in) cake tins, lined

28cm (11in) cake drum, turntable and dowels (optional)

Straight-edge and zig-zag scraper

1 First make the **CREME EGG FILLING** using the quantities listed here, following the method on page 22. Set aside.

2 Preheat the oven to 180°C (160°C fan/350°F/Gas 4).

3 Follow steps 2–4 of the **CLASSIC VICTORIA SPONGE** recipe (see page 59) to make the sponge batter. Divide the batter between two bowls and colour one with orange gel food colouring.

4 Load each batter into a piping bag and pipe thick alternate vertical lines into the lined cake tins, filling them equally. Using an angled spatula or knife, drag the batter horizontally to create a feathered pattern. Bake in the preheated oven for 30–35 minutes, or until the sponge bounces back when pressed or a knife tip inserted into the middle comes out clean.

5 Let the cakes cool in the tins for 5–10 minutes, then carefully turn out onto wire racks to cool completely.

Filling and stacking

6 Make a batch of **CHOCOLATE BUTTERCREAM** using the quantities listed here (see page 16 for method).

7 Follow the instructions on assembling a one-tier cake with filling (see pages 34–35) to level and stack the cake using the chocolate buttercream and Creme Egg filling.

8 Dowel the cake using the method on page 35 (optional).

9 Chill the cake in the fridge for 30 minutes until the buttercream has solidified, then continue following the crumb coating technique on page 39, with the remaining buttercream. Chill for 30 minutes, or until you are ready to decorate. Save the rest of the chocolate buttercream for the fault line. ▶

Decoration

10 Make a large batch of **VANILLA BUTTERCREAM** using the quantities listed on page 103 for the butter and icing sugar, adding the vanilla extract to taste and the whitening powder, if using (see page 16 for method).

11 Divide the mixture in half and colour one portion orange using gel food colouring. Load each buttercream into a piping bag and follow the ombre technique (see page 46) using just two colours, blending the white to orange. Save any unused or excess buttercream for later.

12 Use the remaining chocolate buttercream from the crumb coat to create a fault line on the bottom half of the cake (see page 44). Finish the fault line with a textured scraper – we used a zig-zag scraper for this cake.

13 Apply a milk chocolate drip of your choice (see page 50). Chill the cake in the fridge for 15 minutes until the drip has set.

14 Load a piping bag with your nozzle of choice and the rest of the chocolate, orange, white and mixed buttercream using the multi-tone piping method (see page 24). Cover the top of the cake and around the cake drum using the classic rosette technique (see page 26). Return to the fridge until the day you are cutting the cake.

15 Before serving, decorate with chocolates, gold leaf, Creme Eggs, sprinkles and edible glitter.

CREME EGG CUPCAKES & JARS

INGREDIENTS

Makes 12 cupcakes / 4 cake jars

180g (1½ sticks) unsalted butter

180g (¾ cup plus 2 tbsp) caster sugar

3 eggs

180g (1½ cups) self-raising flour

Orange gel food colouring

Buttercream

200g (1 stick plus 5 tbsp) unsalted butter

350g (3 cups) icing sugar

Orange gel food colouring

50g (½ cup) cocoa powder

Filling

12 tsp Creme Egg Filling
(see page 22)

Decoration

Cadbury's Creme Eggs

SPECIAL EQUIPMENT

Mixer or hand-held electric whisk

12-hole cupcake tin, lined with cases

Piping bag and Rachel #2D or Emily #1E nozzle (or nozzle of choice)

> **TOP TIP ★** We recommend making a full batch of Creme Egg Filling to keep on-hand, stored in the fridge, rather than making small batches for cupcakes and jars.

1   Use the quantities listed here for the butter, sugar, eggs and flour to make the cupcake batter, following the method in steps 1–4 of the **CLASSIC VICTORIA SPONGE** recipe (see page 59). Divide the batter in half and colour one portion orange.

2   Spoon a mix of orange and plain batter into each cupcake case, until each one is just over half-filled. Use a toothpick to swirl the colours together slightly.

3   Bake in the preheated oven for 15–20 minutes, or until the cupcakes bounce back when pressed. Leave to cool on a wire rack.

4   Make a batch of **PLAIN BUTTERCREAM** (see page 16 for method) using the quantities listed here. Divide it between three bowls. Colour one portion orange, leave one plain and add the cocoa powder to the third.

5   Core the cupcakes (see page 29) and use a teaspoon to fill each one with the **CREME EGG FILLING**. Replace the tops.

6   Follow the multi-tone piping technique (see page 24) to load the coloured buttercreams into a piping bag fitted with your nozzle of choice and pipe onto the cupcakes in a classic rosette or swirl (see page 26). Top each with half or a quarter of a Creme Egg.

To make cake jars

Follow the method above to make 12 Creme Egg cupcakes (undecorated) and the buttercream. You will need 3 cupcakes or 150g (5oz) of cake per jar.

We recommend including thin layers of melted chocolate spread, as well as the buttercream and Creme Egg filling.

Fill the jars in layers using the cake jar tutorial on page 55.

VANILLA & CHOCOLATE HALF & HALF CAKE

Over the years, we have developed and perfected our half and half cakes – from the thrown together piles of sponge they originated as in 2016, to the almost seamless and meticulously stacked fusion of flavours they have gloriously become.

INGREDIENTS

Makes a 20cm (8in), 4-layer cake

Victoria sponge half

300g (2½ sticks) unsalted butter

300g (1½ cups) caster sugar

5 eggs

300g (2¼ cups) self-raising flour

Vanilla buttercream

125g (1 stick) unsalted butter

250g (1¾ cups) icing sugar

½ tsp vanilla extract

Filling

Strawberry or raspberry jam

Decoration

250g (2 sticks) unsalted butter

500g (3½ cups) icing sugar

1 tsp vanilla extract

1 tsp whitening powder (optional)

Pink, orange, yellow, green, blue and purple gel food colouring

3 tsp white chocolate spread, melted, for the drip

Sprinkles, edible gold leaf and edible glitter pump

White chocolate shards, made from 300g (10oz) white chocolate and some pink oil-based food colouring (see page 32)

Chocolate sponge half

300g (2½ sticks) unsalted butter

300g (1½ cups) caster sugar

5 eggs

100ml (6½ tbsp) boiling water

1 tsp fine instant coffee

50ml (3½ tbsp) vegetable oil

250g (scant 2 cups) self-raising flour

50g (½ cup) cocoa powder

Chocolate buttercream

125g (1 stick) unsalted butter

225g (1⅔ cups) icing sugar

25g (¼ cup) cocoa powder

A dash of vanilla extract

Filling

6 tbsp chocolate spread (optional)

Decoration

250g (2 sticks) unsalted butter

450g (3¼ cups) icing sugar

Up to 50g (½ cup) cocoa powder

3 tsp milk chocolate spread, melted, for the drip

Sprinkles, edible gold leaf and edible glitter pump

About 5 pieces of Milk Chocolate Rocky Road (see page 190)

SPECIAL EQUIPMENT

Mixer or hand-held electric whisk

4 x 20cm (8in) cake tins, lined

Cake drum, turntable and dowels (optional)

Thick stripe scraper and zig-zag scraper

Piping bags and nozzles of your choice

▶

1   Preheat the oven to 180°C (160°C fan/350°F/Gas 4).

2   Follow steps 2–4 of the **CLASSIC VICTORIA SPONGE** recipe (see page 59), using the quantities listed here for the Victoria sponge half. Divide the mixture between two lined cake tins. Set aside.

3   Follow steps 2–3 of the **CLASSIC VICTORIA SPONGE** recipe (see page 59), using the quantities listed here for the chocolate sponge half. Pour the boiling water into a mug and stir in the instant coffee. Add this and the vegetable oil to the batter, and combine. Sift the flour and cocoa powder into the mixture and fold in using a spatula or a low speed setting on a mixer – do not overmix. Divide the chocolate batter between the remaining two lined cake tins.

4   Bake all four cakes in the preheated oven for 30–35 minutes, or until the sponge bounces back when pressed. You can check by inserting a sharp knife into the centre; if it comes out clean, the cake is ready.

5   Let the sponges cool for 5–10 minutes in the tins, then carefully turn them out onto wire racks and leave to cool completely.

Filling and stacking

6   Make a batch of **VANILLA BUTTERCREAM** and a batch of **CHOCOLATE BUTTERCREAM** using the quantities listed on page 106 (see page 16 for method).

7   Refer to the half and half technique (see page 52) to level and stack the cake using strawberry or raspberry jam and the vanilla buttercream on the vanilla half, and the chocolate spread (if using) and chocolate buttercream on the chocolate half.

8   Dowel the cake using the method on page 35 (optional).

9   Chill the cake in the fridge for 30 minutes until the buttercream has solidified. Crumb coat the cake (see page 39) with the remaining buttercreams, using the correct flavour for each side. Chill for a further 30 minutes, or until you are ready to decorate.

Decoration

10 For the vanilla half, make a batch of **VANILLA BUTTERCREAM** (see page 16). Set aside one half (this is for decorating the top – add whitening powder, if you like).

11 Divide the other half of the buttercream equally among 6 bowls. Colour them pink, orange, yellow, green, blue and purple. Follow the rainbow stripes technique on page 43, only covering the vanilla half of the cake in the striped buttercream – it will not matter that there is not a straight line yet.

12 Refer to the half and half technique (see page 52) to use two pieces of baking parchment to create a stencil for straight lines down the each side of the cake, where the flavours meet.

13 For the chocolate half, make a batch of **PLAIN BUTTERCREAM** using the quantities listed on page 106 for the butter and icing sugar. Divide the buttercream among three bowls and use the cocoa powder to make three different shades of chocolate buttercream.

14 Apply the buttercream referring to the ombre technique on page 46, overlapping the baking parchment. Save any remaining buttercream to decorate the top of the cake.

15 Scrape the chocolate buttercream half with a straight-edge scraper to smooth it, and finish using a zig-zag scraper. Place the cake in the fridge for 10–15 minutes.

16 Prepare your preferred drip method (see page 50) – we have used melted milk chocolate and white chocolate spread and added sprinkles and gold leaf.

17 Load a piping bag with your chosen nozzle and the vanilla buttercream, then pipe small swirls over the vanilla half of the cake and the cake drum. Repeat using the chocolate buttercream on the chocolate half of the cake.

18 Cut the milk chocolate rocky road into bite-sized pieces and use to decorate the chocolate side of the cake. Decorate the vanilla side with the white chocolate shards. Finish with edible glitter.

19 Chill in the fridge for a couple of hours, or until the day you are cutting the cake.

COOKIES & COOKIE CUPS

CHEWY CHOCOLATE CHIP COOKIES

These two simple, chewy chocolate chip cookie recipes are used as the base for several of the recipes throughout this book. They can be served warm with ice cream or enjoyed cold. With no need to chill the dough, this quick and easy recipe is a staple recipe for any baker.

INGREDIENTS

Makes 12

180g (1½ sticks) unsalted butter, melted

150g (¾ cup) granulated sugar

150g (¾ cup packed) light soft brown sugar

1 egg plus 1 egg yolk

45g (3 tbsp) golden syrup

300g (2⅓ cups) plain flour

1 tsp baking powder

150g (5oz) white chocolate chips, plus extra for the tops

150g (5oz) milk chocolate chips, plus extra for the tops

SPECIAL EQUIPMENT

Mixer or hand-held electric whisk

Small ice cream scoop (optional)

2–3 baking trays, lined

1 Preheat the oven to 180°C (160°C fan/350°F/Gas 4).

2 Mix together the melted butter, both sugars, the egg and egg yolk, and mix with a spoon until combined.

3 Add to the mixer bowl (if using; this can also be done with a hand-held electric whisk) and add the golden syrup, flour and baking powder. Mix on a medium speed until combined, then add the chocolate chips and mix again. The mixture should be quite wet and sticky-looking, so leave it for 5 minutes to settle.

4 Using a small ice cream scoop or your hands, ball the mixture into 12 small balls (around 75g/2½oz per cookie).

5 Arrange on the lined baking trays. Add extra chocolate chips to the top of the cookie dough balls, then bake in the preheated oven for 10–12 minutes, or until the edges are golden brown.

6 Tap the baking trays onto a counter or table a couple of times to knock the air out of the cookies – they should deflate slightly when you do this. Leave to cool completely on the trays as they will continue to cook after they come out of the oven.

To make chewy double chocolate chip cookies

Replace 50g (½ cup) of the flour with cocoa powder, and use 300g (10oz) of milk or dark chocolate chips instead of the white and milk chocolate chips.

CHUNKY CHOCOLATE CHIP COOKIES

These are our thick, gooey, chocolate-stuffed, ultimate chocolate chip cookies. Eat cold or, better still, warmed through in the microwave at full power for 30 seconds for that New York-style bakery goodness. These have a lot of chocolate in, so reduce the quantity if you like. Use a mixture of chocolate chips that will stay solid (bake-stable) and some that melt for an even more indulgent texture.

INGREDIENTS

Makes 12

250g (2 sticks) unsalted butter

125g (⅔ cup) granulated sugar

175g (¾ cup plus 2 tbsp packed) light soft brown sugar

2 eggs plus 1 egg yolk

600g (4⅔ cups) plain flour

10g (1 tbsp) cornflour

2 tsp baking powder

½ tsp bicarbonate of soda

½ tsp salt

1 tsp vanilla extract

500g (18oz) milk chocolate chips, plus extra for the middles and tops

SPECIAL EQUIPMENT

Mixer or hand-held electric whisk

2–3 baking trays, lined

1   Place the butter in a mixer (or use a hand-held electric whisk) and mix on medium speed until smooth and light in colour.

2   Add both sugars, the eggs and egg yolk, and beat together until combined.

3   Add the rest of the ingredients and combine everything together.

4   Weigh out each cookie at 150g (5oz) each and roll into balls. Split each ball in half and press some extra chocolate chips into the middle. Press the two halves back together and roll into a firm ball. Arrange the cookies on the lined baking trays.

5   Press some more chocolate chips into the top of each cookie and then chill the cookies in the fridge for 30 minutes. Meanwhile, preheat the oven to 220°C (200°C fan/425°F/Gas 7).

6   Once chilled, bake the cookies in the preheated oven for 12 minutes. The cookies shouldn't spread much, so they can be squashed slightly before baking if they are too chilled.

7   Allow to cool completely on the trays.

To make chunky double chocolate chip cookies

Replace 50g (½ cup) of the flour with cocoa powder.

PUMPKIN SPICE COOKIES

Whether you like it in your latte or prefer a sweeter treat, pumpkin spice is an autumn staple. Filled with a soft cream cheese centre, these cookies will have you dreaming about cosy nights in.

INGREDIENTS

Makes 12

250g (2 sticks) unsalted butter

125g (⅔ cup) granulated sugar

175g (¾ cup plus 2 tbsp packed) light soft brown sugar

2 eggs plus 1 egg yolk

600g (4⅔ cups) plain flour

10g (1 tbsp) cornflour

2 tsp baking powder

½ tsp bicarbonate of soda

½ tsp salt

1 tsp vanilla extract

Orange oil-based or gel food colouring

2½ tsp Pumpkin Spice Mix (see page 23)

200g (7oz) milk chocolate chips

200g (7oz) white chocolate chips, plus 150g (5oz) to decorate

Pumpkin seeds, to decorate (optional)

Cream cheese filling

80g (3oz) full-fat cream cheese

200g (1¾ cups) icing sugar

2 tbsp cornflour

A dash of lemon juice

SPECIAL EQUIPMENT

Mixer or hand-held electric whisk

2–3 baking trays, lined

1 Make the **CREAM CHEESE FILLING** using the quantities listed here and following the method on page 20. The consistency should be like thick glacé icing. If the mixture is too runny, add 50g (⅓ cup) icing sugar at a time until it reaches the right consistency. Put the mixture into the freezer for 30 minutes to solidify slightly.

2 Follow steps 1–3 of the **CHUNKY CHOCOLATE CHIP COOKIES** recipe (see page 114) using the quantities listed here, adding some orange food colouring and the pumpkin spice mix before adding the flour, and adding the milk and white chocolate chips.

3 Form 12 even balls of cookie dough, weighing around 140g (4½oz) each. Split each ball in half. Flatten both halves slightly against the work surface with your palm. Put one half in your hand and, using a teaspoon, dollop the cream cheese filling in the centre of the dough. Carefully pick up the other flattened half with the other hand and place over the top. Pinch the sides together making sure no cream cheese filling escapes. Roll gently in your hands to seal.

4 Once all 12 cookies are filled and rolled into a thick cookie shape, add the white chocolate chips and some pumpkin seeds, if using, to the tops.

5 Arrange the cookies on the lined baking trays and place in the fridge for a minimum of 30 minutes.

6 Preheat the oven to 220°C (200°C fan/425°F/Gas 7).

7 Bake in the preheated oven for 12 minutes. Leave to cool completely on the trays.

TOP TIP ★ Roll in cinnamon sugar before baking (1:1 ground cinnamon and granulated sugar) for an extra sweet crunch.

RED VELVET STUFFED COOKIES

Red velvet is the perfect balance of chocolate and vanilla accompanied by tangy but sweet cream cheese, and is beautifully red! Our cookie version of the traditional cake is stuffed with white chocolate chips and a melt-in-the-mouth cream cheese filling.

INGREDIENTS

Makes 12

250g (2 sticks) unsalted butter

125g (⅔ cup) granulated sugar

175g (¾ cup plus 2 tbsp) light soft brown sugar

2 eggs plus 1 egg yolk

¼ tsp red gel food colouring *(we use Sugarflair Red Extra)*

1 tsp vanilla extract

600g (4⅔ cups) plain flour

10g (1 tbsp) cornflour

2 tsp baking powder

½ tsp bicarbonate of soda

½ tsp salt

25g (¼ cup) cocoa powder

400g (14oz) white chocolate chips, plus 150g (5oz) for the tops

Cream cheese filling

80g (3oz) full-fat cream cheese

200g (1¾ cups) icing sugar, plus extra if needed

2 tbsp cornflour

A dash of lemon juice

SPECIAL EQUIPMENT

Mixer or hand-held electric whisk

2–3 baking trays, lined

1 Make the **CREAM CHEESE FILLING** using the quantities listed here and following the method on page 20. The consistency should be like thick glacé icing; if the mixture is too runny, add 50g (⅓ cup) icing sugar at a time until you reach the right consistency. Put the mixture into the freezer for 30 minutes to solidify slightly. It will not freeze completely.

2 For the cookies, place the butter in a mixer (or use a hand-held electric whisk) and mix on medium speed until smooth and light in colour.

3 Add both sugars, the eggs, egg yolk and red food colouring, and beat until combined.

4 Mix in the rest of the ingredients apart from the chocolate chips. When the dough has formed, add the chocolate chips.

5 Remove the cream cheese from the freezer. Weigh out 12 balls of cookie dough, 150g (5oz) each. Split each ball in half and flatten both halves slightly against the work surface with your palm. Put one half back in your hand and, using a teaspoon, dollop the cream cheese filling onto the centre of the dough. Carefully pick up the other flattened half with the other hand and place on top. Pinch the sides together so no cream cheese filling escapes. Roll gently again in your hands to seal.

6 Once all 12 cookies are filled and rolled into a thick cookie shape, add extra white chocolate chips to the tops. Arrange the cookies on the lined baking trays.

7 Chill the cookies in the fridge for at least 30 minutes. Meanwhile, preheat the oven to 220°C (200°C fan/425°F/Gas 7).

8 Bake in the preheated oven for 12 minutes. Take out and leave to cool completely on the trays.

NUTELLA STUFFED COOKIES

Our original double chocolate cookie with a gooey Nutella centre. This chocolate chip cookie recipe is so versatile, you can leave it plain or stuff with any chocolate spread you like. Warm up for 30 seconds in the microwave at full power once cooled, or better still eat warm from the oven. These cookies do not last for very long in our bakery – our team take some home most days too!

INGREDIENTS

Makes 12

12 tbsp Nutella

250g (2 sticks) unsalted butter

125g (⅔ cup) granulated sugar

175g (¾ cup plus 2 tbsp packed) light soft brown sugar

2 eggs plus 1 egg yolk

550g (4⅓ cups) plain flour

50g (½ cup) cocoa powder

10g (1 tbsp) cornflour

2 tsp baking powder

½ tsp bicarbonate of soda

½ tsp salt

500g (18oz) milk chocolate chips, plus extra for the tops

1 tsp vanilla extract

SPECIAL EQUIPMENT

2–3 baking trays, lined

Mixer or hand-held electric whisk

1 Spoon 12 individually heaped tablespoons of Nutella onto a lined baking tray and place in the freezer for a couple of hours until frozen. These will be the fillings for the cookies.

2 Preheat the oven to 220°C (200°C fan/425°F/Gas 7).

3 Follow steps 1–3 of the **CHUNKY DOUBLE CHOCOLATE CHIP COOKIES** recipe (see page 114), using the quantities listed here.

4 Weigh the cookie dough into 12 portions of 150g (5oz) each, and roll into balls. Split each ball in half and press a ball of frozen Nutella into the middle. Press the two halves back together again and roll into a firm ball.

5 Place the balls onto the lined baking trays and flatten them slightly. Add chocolate chips to the tops of the cookies. Bake in the preheated oven for 12 minutes. (If you are baking in batches, put them in the fridge until they are ready to be baked.) Leave to cool completely on the trays.

TOP TIP ★ Freezing blobs of Nutella will allow the cookie to maintain its centre, and not just leak out whilst cooking. Freeze the spoonfuls of Nutella in advance and keep them in the freezer until needed.

LOTUS BISCOFF STUFFED COOKIES

Another variation of our classic chunky cookie, these stuffed cookies are filled to the brim with crushed Lotus Biscoff biscuits. When eaten warmed up or, even better, fresh out of the oven, they ooze that gorgeous golden goodness!

INGREDIENTS

Makes 12

12 heaped tbsp Lotus Biscoff spread

190g (6½oz) Lotus Biscoff biscuits

250g (2 sticks) unsalted butter

125g (⅔ cup) granulated sugar

175g (¾ cup plus 2 tbsp packed) light soft brown sugar

2 eggs plus 1 egg yolk

600g (4⅔ cups) plain flour

10g (1 tbsp) cornflour

2 tsp baking powder

½ tsp bicarbonate of soda

½ tsp salt

1 tsp vanilla extract

200g (7oz) milk chocolate chips, plus 75g (2½oz) for the tops

200g (7oz) white chocolate chips, plus 75g (2½oz) for the tops

SPECIAL EQUIPMENT

2–3 baking trays

Lined mixer or hand-held electric whisk

1   Spoon 12 individual heaped tablespoons of Lotus Biscoff spread onto a lined baking tray and place in the freezer for a couple of hours until frozen. These will be the fillings for the cookies.

2   Preheat the oven to 220°C (200°C fan/425°F/Gas 7).

3   Blitz the Lotus biscuits in a food processor or place them into a sandwich bag and crush them using a rolling pin.

4   Follow steps 1–3 of the **CHUNKY CHOCOLATE CHIP COOKIES** recipe (see page 114), using the quantities listed here and mixing in 140g (4½oz) of the crushed biscuits using a low speed on your mixer. Reserve the rest of the crushed biscuits for the topping.

5   Weigh the dough into 12 portions of 150g (5oz) each, and roll into balls. Split each ball in half and press a ball of frozen Lotus spread into the middle. Press the two halves back together again and roll into a firm ball.

6   Place onto the baking trays and flatten slightly. Add the extra chocolate chips to the tops and sprinkle over the reserved crushed biscuits. Bake in the preheated oven for 12 minutes. (If you are baking in batches, put them in the fridge until they are ready to be baked.) Leave to cool completely on the trays.

TOP TIP ★ Freezing blobs of Lotus Biscoff spread will allow the cookie to maintain its centre, and it won't just leak out whilst cooking.

COOKIE DOUGH STUFFED COOKIES

This recipe takes our original chunky double chocolate chip cookie and stuffs it with an edible cookie dough centre for extra cookie deliciousness.

INGREDIENTS

Makes 12

1 batch of Edible Cookie Dough (see page 20)

250g (2 sticks) unsalted butter

125g (⅔ cup) granulated sugar

175g (¾ cup plus 2 tbsp packed) light soft brown sugar

2 eggs plus 1 egg yolk

550g (4¼ cups) plain flour

50g (½ cup) cocoa powder

10g (1 tbsp) cornflour

2 tsp baking powder

½ tsp bicarbonate of soda

½ tsp salt

1 tsp vanilla extract

500g (18oz) milk chocolate chips, plus extra for the top

SPECIAL EQUIPMENT

Mixer or hand-held electric whisk

2–3 baking trays, lined

1 Roll the **EDIBLE COOKIE DOUGH** into 12 equal-sized balls. Put in the freezer for at least 1 hour.

2 Preheat the oven to 220°C (200°C fan/425°F/Gas 7).

3 Follow steps 1–3 of the **CHUNKY DOUBLE CHOCOLATE CHIP COOKIES** recipe (see page 114), using the quantities listed here.

4 Take the frozen cookie dough balls out the freezer. Weigh the chunky double chocolate chip cookie dough into 12 portions of 150g (5oz) each, and roll into balls. Split each ball in half and press a ball of frozen cookie dough into the middle. Press the two halves back together and roll into a firm ball.

5 Place the balls onto the lined baking trays and flatten them slightly. Add chocolate chips to the tops of the cookies. Bake in the preheated oven for 12 minutes. (If you are baking in batches, put them in the fridge until they are ready to be baked.) Leave to cool completely on the trays.

S'MORES COOKIES

S'mores flavour without the campfire taste. These melted, gooey and sticky cookies combine marshmallows, digestive biscuits (instead of the American Graham crackers) and chocolate, and they will have you licking your fingers long after they've been eaten whilst dreaming of camping in the sunshine.

INGREDIENTS

Makes 12

250g (2 sticks) unsalted butter, softened

125g (⅔ cup) granulated sugar

175g (¾ cup plus 2 tbsp) light soft brown sugar

2 eggs plus 1 egg yolk

600g (4⅔ cups) plain flour

10g (1 tbsp) cornflour

2 tsp baking powder

½ tsp bicarbonate of soda

½ tsp salt

1½ tsp ground cinnamon, or to taste

1 tsp vanilla extract

500g (18oz) milk chocolate chips, plus extra for the tops

100g (2 cups) mini marshmallows, plus 60g (generous ¼ cup) for the middles

6 digestive biscuits, halved

Cinnamon sugar

2 tsp ground cinnamon

20g (5 tsp) granulated sugar

2 digestive biscuits, crushed

SPECIAL EQUIPMENT

Mixer or hand-held electric whisk

2–3 baking trays, lined

1 Follow steps 1–3 of the **CHUNKY CHOCOLATE CHIP COOKIES** recipe (see page 114) using the quantities listed here, but when adding the dry ingredients, add the cinnamon, too.

2 Add the marshmallows to the cookie dough and mix on a very low speed setting until evenly distributed. This will prevent the marshmallows from tearing.

3 Weigh out each cookie at 150g (5oz) each and roll into balls. Split each ball in half and press some more mini marshmallows into the middle. Add ½ a digestive biscuit, press the two halves back together and roll into a firm ball. Pinch the cookie dough sides together making sure no marshmallows escape. Roll gently again in your hands to seal.

4 Mix the cinnamon and granulated sugar together to make the cinnamon sugar, and add the crushed digestive biscuits. Roll each cookie in the mix and top with more chocolate chips.

5 Chill the cookies in the fridge for 30 minutes. Meanwhile, preheat the oven to 220°C (200°C fan/425°F/Gas 7).

6 Once chilled, bake the cookies in the preheated oven for 12 minutes. The cookies shouldn't spread much, so they can be squashed slightly before baking if they are too chilled.

7 Allow to cool completely on the trays.

8 Enjoy warmed up, like you've just melted them over an open fire – without the burn and smoke taste, of course.

GIANT PERSONALIZED COOKIE

Personalize your own giant chewy chocolate chip cookie with this quick and easy recipe. These make perfect presents and can be decorated as you like for celebrations of all kinds.

INGREDIENTS

Makes 1

60g (½ stick) unsalted butter

75g (⅓ cup plus 1 tbsp) granulated sugar

75g (⅓ cup plus 1 tbsp packed) light soft brown sugar

1 egg

17g (1 tbsp) golden syrup

100g (¾ cup) plain flour

⅓ tsp baking powder

100g (3½oz) milk chocolate chips, plus 30g (1oz) for the top

Vanilla buttercream

100g (6½ tbsp) unsalted butter

200g (1¾ cups) icing sugar

1 tsp vanilla extract

Gel or oil-based food colouring

Decoration

Sprinkles and edible glitter

SPECIAL EQUIPMENT

Mixer or hand-held electric whisk

20cm (8in) loose-bottomed cake tin, lined

Piping bag and nozzles of your choice (we used Tessa #348 and writing tip Mandy #R3)

1   Preheat the oven to 180°C (160°C fan/350°F/Gas 4).

2   Follow steps 2–3 of the **CHEWY CHOCOLATE CHIP COOKIES** recipe (see page 113) using the quantities listed here.

3   Press the cookie dough evenly into the base of the lined tin and scatter the 30g (1oz) of extra chocolate chips over the top.

4   Bake in the preheated oven for 14 minutes, or until the edges are golden brown. Tap onto a table or work surface a couple of times to knock the air out of the cookie; it will deflate slightly. Leave to cool completely in the tin.

5   Make a small batch of **VANILLA BUTTERCREAM** (see page 16) using the quantities listed here and your colour or colours of your choice. Pipe flowers, hearts, intricate piping, names or messages onto the cookie and adorn with sprinkles and edible glitter.

TOP TIP ★ If you want to make a thicker cookie, just double the recipe and bake for a couple of minutes longer until the edges are golden brown.

WHITE CHOCOLATE GANACHE COOKIE SANDWICHES

Two of our chewy chocolate chip cookies sandwiched together with melt-in-the-mouth white chocolate ganache and rolled in sprinkles for an extra special touch – yum!

INGREDIENTS

Makes 6

180g (1½ sticks) unsalted butter, melted

150g (¾ cup) granulated sugar

150g (¾ cup packed) light soft brown sugar

1 egg plus 1 egg yolk

45g (3 tbsp) golden syrup

300g (2⅓ cups) plain flour

1 tsp baking powder

150g (5oz) white chocolate chips, plus extra for the top

150g (5oz) milk chocolate chips, plus extra for the top

Ganache

75ml (⅓ cup) double cream

225g (8oz) white chocolate

Decoration

Sprinkles (optional) or other decoration of choice

SPECIAL EQUIPMENT

Mixer or hand-held electric whisk

Small ice cream scoop

2–3 baking trays, lined

Piping bag and #2D Emily or #1E Rachel nozzle (or nozzle of choice)

1. Make the **WHITE CHOCOLATE GANACHE** filling using the quantities listed here, following the method on page 19. Leave to set in the fridge for a couple of hours or at room temperature for 4 hours.

2. Follow steps 1–6 of the **CHEWY CHOCOLATE CHIP COOKIES** recipe (see page 113) to make 12 cookies. Leave to cool and pair up similar-sized cookies together to make 6 cookie sandwiches.

3. Once the ganache has set, use the whisk attachment of a mixer (or use a hand-held electric whisk) to whip until the consistency is like dense whipped cream. If the ganache is too stiff, add some warm cream, a dash at a time. If the ganache is too runny, put it back into the fridge for a while before you whip it again.

4. Transfer the ganache into a piping bag fitted with your nozzle of choice.

5. Pipe a large, classic rosette (see page 26) with medium pressure about 1cm (½in) in from the edge of one cookie. Press the paired cookie onto the ganache and squeeze gently.

6. Turn the cookie sandwich on its side and sprinkle on the decoration of your choice. Repeat to make the remaining cookie sandwiches.

TOP TIP ★ Use half a small scoop of cookie dough to make smaller, bite-sized cookie sandwiches.

MILK CHOCOLATE GANACHE COOKIE SANDWICHES

A counter-part for our white chocolate ganache cookie sandwich, this will divide the milk chocolate from the white chocolate lovers. If you're a fan of both, why not try using one chocolate chip cookie, one double chocolate chip cookie and swirl together with both milk and white chocolate ganache?

INGREDIENTS

Makes 6

180g (1½ sticks) unsalted butter

150g (¾ cup) granulated sugar

150g (¾ cup packed) light soft brown sugar

1 egg plus 1 egg yolk

250g (scant 2 cups) plain flour

50g (½ cup) cocoa powder

1 tsp baking powder

45g (3 tbsp) golden syrup

300g (10oz) milk chocolate chips, plus extra for the top

Milk chocolate ganache

125ml (½ cup) double cream

225g (8oz) milk chocolate

Decoration

Chocolate curls (optional) or other decoration of choice

SPECIAL EQUIPMENT

Mixer or hand-held electric whisk

Small ice cream scoop

2–3 baking trays, lined

Piping bag and #2D Emily or #1E Rachel nozzle (or nozzle of choice)

1 Make the **MILK CHOCOLATE GANACHE** filling using the quantities listed here, following the method on page 19. Leave to set in the fridge for a couple of hours or at room temperature for 4 hours.

2 Follow steps 1–6 of the **CHEWY DOUBLE CHOCOLATE CHIP COOKIES** recipe (see page 113) to make 12 cookies. Leave to cool and then pair up similar-sized cookies together to make 6 cookie sandwiches.

3 Once the ganache has set, use the whisk attachment of a mixer (or use a hand-held electric whisk) to whip until the consistency is like dense whipped cream. If the ganache is too stiff, add some warm cream, a dash at a time. If the ganache is too runny, put it back into the fridge for a while before you whip it again.

4 Transfer the ganache into a piping bag fitted with your nozzle of choice.

5 Pipe a large, classic rosette (see page 26) with medium pressure about 1cm (½in) in from the edge of one cookie. Press the paired cookie onto the ganache and squeeze gently.

6 Turn the cookie sandwich on its side and sprinkle on the decoration of your choice – for these we chose chocolate curls. Repeat to make the remaining cookie sandwiches.

RASPBERRY & WHITE CHOCOLATE GANACHE COOKIE SANDWICHES

Is this the best-tasting thing since our original ganache cookie sandwiches? Yes, and it's pink! Creamy, pink, raspberry-flavoured ganache, sandwiched between two white chocolate cookies, rolled in chocolate curls and freeze-dried raspberries, and finished with edible glitter – heaven!

INGREDIENTS

Makes 6

180g (1½ sticks) unsalted butter

150g (¾ cup) granulated sugar

150g (¾ cup packed) light soft brown sugar

1 egg plus 1 egg yolk

45g (3 tbsp) golden syrup

300g (2⅓ cups) plain flour

1 tsp baking powder

300g (10oz) white chocolate chips, plus extra for the top

White chocolate ganache

150g (⅔ cup) double cream

450g (1lb) white chocolate

Oil-based pink food colouring

A few drops of raspberry flavouring

Filling

6 tsp raspberry jam

Decoration

Freeze-dried raspberry pieces and white chocolate curls, or other decoration of choice

SPECIAL EQUIPMENT

Mixer or hand-held electric whisk

Small ice cream scoop

2–3 baking trays, lined

Piping bag and #2D Emily or #1E Rachel nozzle (or nozzle of choice)

1   Start with the white chocolate ganache for the filling. Make a **WHITE CHOCOLATE GANACHE** with the double cream and white chocolate following the method on page 19. Leave to set in the fridge for a couple of hours or at room temperature for 4 hours.

2   Follow steps 1–6 of the **CHEWY CHOCOLATE CHIP COOKIES** recipe (see page 113) using the quantities listed here and using white chocolate chips only, to make 12 cookies. Pair up similar-sized cookies together to make 6 cookie sandwiches.

3   Once the ganache has set, use the whisk attachment of a mixer (or hand-held electric whisk) to whip until the consistency is like dense whipped cream. If the ganache is too stiff, add some warm cream, a dash at a time. If the ganache is too runny, put it back into the fridge for a while before you whip it again. Add in a little oil-based food colouring and a few drops of raspberry flavouring to taste. Put the ganache into a piping bag fitted with your nozzle of choice.

4   Spread a teaspoonful of raspberry jam on the very centre of one of the cookies, making sure it is not spread too close to the edge.

5   Pipe a large, classic rosette (see page 26) of ganache, using medium pressure, about 1cm (½in) in from the edge of the cookie, making sure to encase the jam. This is important as the ganache will solidify around the jam which will minimize the chance of the jam seeping out. Press the paired cookie onto the ganache and squeeze gently.

6   Turn the cookie sandwich on its side and sprinkle on the decoration of your choice. For these, we have used freeze-dried raspberry pieces and white chocolate curls. Repeat to make the remaining cookie sandwiches.

DARK CHOCOLATE & SEA SALT GANACHE COOKIE SANDWICHES

Sea salt complements the rich taste of dark chocolate beautifully, and these cookie sandwiches are no exception. We've added a caramel centre to these cookie sandwiches and topped them with salt flakes – a divine combination of sweet and salty.

INGREDIENTS

Makes 6

180g (1½ sticks) unsalted butter

150g (¾ cup) granulated sugar

150g (¾ cup packed) light soft brown sugar

1 egg plus 1 egg yolk

45g (3 tbsp) golden syrup

250g (scant 2 cups) plain flour

50g (½ cup) cocoa powder

1 tsp baking powder

300g (10oz) dark chocolate chips, plus extra for the top

Sea salt, to taste

Dark chocolate ganache

200ml (scant 1 cup) double cream

400g (14oz) dark chocolate

Salted caramel filling

100g (½ cup) Salted Caramel (see page 21)

Decoration

Melted dark chocolate, to drizzle

Sprinkles and sea salt

SPECIAL EQUIPMENT

Mixer or hand-held electric whisk

Small ice cream scoop

2–3 baking trays, lined

Piping bag and #2D Emily or #1E Rachel nozzle (or nozzle of choice)

1 Make the **DARK CHOCOLATE GANACHE** using the quantities listed here, following the method on page 19. Leave to set in the fridge for a couple of hours or at room temperature for 4 hours.

2 Follow steps 1–6 of the **CHEWY DOUBLE CHOCOLATE CHIP COOKIES** recipe (see page 113) to make 12 cookies, adding a pinch of sea salt to the top of each cookie before baking. Leave to cool and pair up similar-sized cookies together to make 6 cookie sandwiches.

3 Once the ganache has set, use the whisk attachment on a mixer (or use a hand-held electric whisk) to whip it until the consistency is like dense whipped cream. If the ganache is too stiff, add some warm cream, a dash at a time; if the ganache is too runny, put it back into the fridge for a while before you whip it again.

4 Make a batch of **SALTED CARAMEL** (see page 21) and pipe or spoon a blob into the centre of half of the cookies, making sure it is not spread too close to the edge.

5 Load the ganache into a piping bag fitted with your nozzle of choice. Pipe a large, classic rosette (see page 26) with medium pressure about 1cm (½in) in from the edge of one cookie, making sure to encase the caramel. This is important as the ganache will solidify around the caramel which will minimize the chance of the caramel seeping out. Press the paired cookie onto the ganache and squeeze gently. Repeat to make the remaining cookie sandwiches.

6 Drizzle with melted dark chocolate. We have decorated these with sprinkles and more salt!

TOP TIP ★ Salt also works well with milk chocolate, if you prefer it to use it instead of dark chocolate.

RED VELVET COOKIE SANDWICHES

With the main components of a classic red velvet cake, this one of our favourite cookie twists. Swirled cream cheese buttercream fills this vibrant red cookie sandwich – it is a perfect taste and colour combination for Valentine's Day.

INGREDIENTS

Makes 6

180g (1½ sticks) unsalted butter

150g (¾ cup) granulated sugar

150g (¾ cup packed) light soft brown sugar

1 egg plus 1 yolk

275g (2 cups plus 2 tbsp) plain flour

25g (¼ cup) cocoa powder

1 tsp baking powder

45g (3 tbsp) golden syrup

1 tbsp buttermilk

¼ tsp red gel food colouring
(we use Sugarflair Red Extra)

300g (10oz) white chocolate chips, plus extra for the top

Cream cheese buttercream

200g (1¾ sticks) unsalted butter

400g (scant 3 cups) icing sugar

150g (5oz) full-fat cream cheese

A dash of lemon juice

SPECIAL EQUIPMENT

Mixer or hand-held electric whisk

Small ice cream scoop

2–3 baking trays, lined

Piping bag and #2D Emily or #1E Rachel nozzle (or nozzle of choice)

1. Follow steps 1–6 of the **CHEWY CHOCOLATE CHIP COOKIES** recipe (see page 113) using the quantities listed here – adding the cocoa powder, buttermilk, red food colouring and using only white chocolate chips – to make 12 cookies. Leave to cool and pair up similar-sized cookies to make 6 cookie sandwiches.

2. Make **CREAM CHEESE BUTTERCREAM** using the quantities listed here, following the method on page 17.

3. Load the buttercream into a piping bag fitted with your nozzle of choice. Pipe a large, classic rosette (see page 26) with medium pressure about 1cm (½in) in from the edge of one cookie. Press the paired cookie onto the buttercream and squeeze gently to sandwich together. Repeat to make the remaining cookie sandwiches.

FUNFETTI COOKIE CUPS

These are perfect for parties, wedding favours, baby showers, dessert tables or just as a little treat. Filled with chocolate, whipped ganache and sprinkles, these cookie cups are a fun twist on our chewy cookie recipe.

INGREDIENTS

Makes 12

180g (1½ sticks) unsalted butter, melted

150g (¾ cup) granulated sugar

150g (¾ cup packed) light soft brown sugar

1 egg plus 1 egg yolk

300g (2⅓ cups) plain flour

1 tsp baking powder

Pinch of salt

45g (3 tbsp) golden syrup

250g (9oz) white chocolate chips

50g (about ⅔ cup) bake-stable funfetti sprinkles (optional)

White chocolate ganache

85g (⅓ cup) double cream

250g (9oz) white chocolate

Pink gel food colouring

Filling

200g (7oz) white chocolate spread

Pink oil-based or gel food colouring

Mini marshmallows and funfetti sprinkles

Decoration

Melted white chocolate

Sprinkles and sweets

SPECIAL EQUIPMENT

Mixer or hand-held electric whisk

Small ice cream scoop (optional)

12-hole cupcake tin, greased

Piping bag and #R18L Stuart nozzle (or nozzle of choice)

1 Make the **WHITE CHOCOLATE GANACHE** using the quantities listed here, following the method on page 19. Leave to set and cool completely; 2–4 hours depending on the temperature of the room. The texture should look and feel slightly rubbery.

2 Preheat the oven to 190°C (170°C fan/375°F/Gas 5).

3 Follow steps 2–4 of the **CHEWY CHOCOLATE CHIP COOKIES** recipe (see page 113) using the quantities listed here, remembering to include the bake-stable funfetti sprinkles and using white chocolate chips only.

4 Place a ball of dough into each hole of the cupcake tin. It should sit inside the hole and weigh about 75g (2½oz). Make a small indentation with the end of a rolling pin to flatten each ball.

5 Bake for 12–14 minutes, or until the edges of the cookies are golden brown. Take the tin out of the oven and drop several times onto a table – this will knock some air out of the cookies and they will flatten. Leave to settle for 5–10 minutes.

6 Taking the end of a rolling pin, gently press down into the centre of each cookie cup. Move the rolling pin in a circular motion to create a well within the cookie. If the mixture is still too wet, try again in 5 minutes. When a well has been created, leave to cool.

7 Remove the cookie cups by gently twisting them and easing them out. Place on a wire rack. Melt the white chocolate spread and colour it pink. Spoon it into the cookie cups, push mini marshmallows into it and sprinkle more funfetti on top. Let it set.

8 Use the whisk attachment on your mixer (or use a hand-held electric whisk) to whip the ganache until it is white and the consistency of whipping cream. Add food colouring and load it into a piping bag fitted with your nozzle of choice.

9 Hold the tip directly over the middle of each cookie cup and squeeze, creating a dome of ganache. Decorate with a drizzle of melted white chocolate, sprinkles and sweets of your choice.

LOTUS BISCOFF & CARAMEL COOKIE CUPS

A perfectly formed cup, made entirely of baked cookie, filled with caramel and topped with a scoop of Lotus Biscoff ganache. We guarantee cookie cups will be your new favourite bake to experiment with different flavours and fillings!

INGREDIENTS

Makes 12

180g (1½ sticks) unsalted butter, melted

150g (¾ cup) granulated sugar

150g (¾ cup packed) light soft brown sugar

1 egg plus 1 egg yolk

300g (2⅓ cups) plain flour

1 tsp baking powder

Pinch of salt

45g (3 tbsp) golden syrup

250g (9oz) milk chocolate chips

75g (2½oz) Lotus Biscoff biscuits, crushed

White chocolate ganache

85g (⅓ cup) double cream

250g (9oz) white chocolate

75g (5 tbsp) Lotus Biscoff spread

Filling

120g (4oz) caramel
(see page 21 or use store-bought caramel sauce)

12 Maltesers (optional)

Decoration

Lotus Biscoff spread, melted

12 Lotus Biscoff biscuits

SPECIAL EQUIPMENT

Mixer or hand-held electric whisk

Small ice cream scoop (optional)

12-hole cupcake tin, greased

Piping bag and #R18L Stuart nozzle (or nozzle of choice)

1   Make the **WHITE CHOCOLATE GANACHE** using the quantities listed here, following the method on page 19. You will add the Lotus Biscoff spread later. Leave to set and cool completely; 2–4 hours depending on the temperature of the room.

2   Preheat the oven to 190°C (170°C fan/375°F/Gas 5).

3   Follow steps 2–4 of the **CHEWY CHOCOLATE CHIP COOKIES** recipe (see page 113) using the quantities listed here, adding the crushed biscuits and using milk chocolate chips only.

4   Place a ball of dough into each hole of the cupcake tin. It should sit inside the hole and weigh about 75g (2½oz). Make a small indentation with the end of a rolling pin to flatten each ball.

5   Bake for 12–14 minutes until the edges of the cookies are golden brown. Drop several times onto a table to knock some air out of the cookies and they will flatten. Leave to settle for 5–10 minutes.

6   Taking the end of a rolling pin, gently press down into the centre of each cookie cup. Move the rolling pin in a circular motion to create a well within the cookie. If the mixture is still too wet, try again in 5 minutes. When a well has been created, leave to cool.

7   Remove the cookie cups by gently twisting them and easing them out. Place on a wire rack. Spoon a heaped teaspoon of caramel into each cup. Push a Malteser, if using, into the centre.

8   Use the whisk attachment on a mixer (or a hand-held electric whisk) to whip the ganache until it is white and the consistency of whipping cream. Soften the Lotus spread and mix it in. Transfer to a piping bag fitted with your nozzle of choice.

9   Hold the tip directly over the middle of each cookie cup and squeeze, creating a dome of ganache. Decorate with a drizzle of melted Lotus spread, sprinkles and more Lotus biscuits.

COOKIE DOUGH COOKIE CUPS

A chewy cookie cup base is filled to the brim with edible cookie dough and topped with a soft scoop of milk chocolate ganache. What could be better?

INGREDIENTS

Makes 12

180g (1½ sticks) unsalted butter, melted

150g (¾ cup) granulated sugar

150g (¾ cup packed) dark soft brown sugar

1 egg plus 1 egg yolk

45g (3 tbsp) golden syrup

250g (scant 2 cups) plain flour

50g (½ cup) cocoa powder

1 tsp baking powder

300g (10oz) milk or dark chocolate chips

Milk chocolate ganache

85g (⅓ cup) double cream

250g (9oz) milk chocolate

Edible cookie dough

½ batch of Edible Cookie Dough (see page 20)

Decoration

Melted milk chocolate, to drizzle

SPECIAL EQUIPMENT

Mixer or hand-held electric whisk

12-hole cupcake tin, greased

Piping bag and #R18L Stuart nozzle (or nozzle of choice)

TOP TIP ★ This recipe works using both milk and white chocolate ganache, and you can mix and match the cookie base with other cookie cup recipes!

1. Make the **MILK CHOCOLATE GANACHE** using the quantities listed here, following the instructions on page 19. Leave to set until completely cooled; 2–4 hours. When hardening, the texture should look and feel slightly rubbery.

2. Preheat the oven to 190°C (170°C fan/375°F/Gas 5).

3. Follow steps 2–4 of the **CHEWY DOUBLE CHOCOLATE CHIP COOKIES** recipe (see page 113) using the quantities listed here.

4. Place a ball of dough – about 75g (2½oz) – into each greased hole of the cupcake tin; it should just fit inside. Make a small indentation with the end of a rolling pin to flatten each ball.

5. Bake in the preheated oven for 12–14 minutes, or until the edges are golden brown. Take the tin out of the oven and drop several times onto a work surface or table to knock some air out. Leave to settle for 5–10 minutes.

6. Using the end of a rolling pin, gently press down into the centre of each cookie cup. Move the rolling pin in a circular motion to create a well within the cookie. If the mixture is still too wet, try again in 5 minutes. When a well has been created, leave to cool.

7. Remove the cookie cups by gently twisting them, easing them out. Place on a wire rack, then push a small ball of the edible cookie dough into each cup. Reserve the rest for decoration.

8. Once the milk chocolate ganache has slightly hardened, use the whisk attachment on a mixer (or use a hand-held electric whisk) and whip until it is soft and the consistency of whipping cream. Load it into a piping bag fitted with your nozzle of choice.

9. Hold the tip directly over the middle of each cookie cup and squeeze, creating a dome of ganache. Drizzle with melted milk chocolate and top each one with a smaller ball of cookie dough.

PEANUT BUTTER COOKIE PIE

Layers of white and milk chocolate, peanut butter, chewy cookie and chocolate chips, this impressive cookie pie is one for the peanut butter lovers among us.

INGREDIENTS

Serves 12–15

270g (2 sticks plus 2 tbsp) unsalted butter

225g (1 cup plus 2 tbsp) granulated sugar

225g (1 cup plus 2 tbsp packed) light soft brown sugar

1 egg plus 2 yolks

75g (5 tbsp) golden syrup

100g (scant ½ cup) peanut butter

450g (3½ cups) plain flour

1½ tsp baking powder

200g (7oz) milk chocolate chips

200g (1¼ cups) peanut butter chips

Filling

450g (1lb) white chocolate

50ml (3½ tbsp) vegetable oil

150g (scant 1 cup) peanut butter chips

100g (7 tbsp) peanut butter

200g (7oz) milk chocolate

SPECIAL EQUIPMENT

Mixer or hand-held electric whisk

20cm (8in) round cake tin, lined

1 Follow steps 2–3 of the **CHEWY CHOCOLATE CHIP COOKIES** recipe (see page 113) using the quantities listed here, and including the peanut butter and peanut butter chips.

2 Divide the dough in half. Press half the dough into the bottom of the lined tin and up the sides in an even layer. If there is any left, add it to the other portion. Place it in the fridge to chill.

3 For the filling, melt 250g (9oz) of the white chocolate and add the vegetable oil to prevent the chocolate from cracking when cut. Mix together until combined. Pour over the base of the cookie dough. Scatter one-third of the peanut butter chips over the top and return it to the fridge to chill until firm.

4 Melt the remaining 200g (7oz) of white chocolate, this time with half of the peanut butter mixture. Mix until combined.

5 Gently press another thin layer of cookie dough over the hardened white chocolate. Pour over the melted white chocolate and peanut butter, and scatter another third of the peanut butter chips over the top. Return to the fridge until firm.

6 Preheat the oven to 190°C (170°C fan/375°F/Gas 5).

7 Melt the milk chocolate with the remaining peanut butter and mix until combined. When the white chocolate and peanut butter layer has set, add another thin layer of cookie dough, and pour the milk chocolate mixture over the top. Scatter with the remaining peanut butter chips. Return to the fridge until firm.

8 When the chocolate has set, add the final thin layer of cookie dough to the top as a lid.

9 Put the cookie pie into the preheated oven and bake for 30 minutes. Leave to cool completely in the tin before removing and cutting into slices.

TRAY BAKES

CHOCOLATE BROWNIES

Filled with melted chocolate, cocoa and chocolate chips, this thick fudgy brownie recipe is the perfect indulgent treat for brownie lovers. These taste incredible when warmed through, and with a drizzle of double cream and some freshly cut strawberries.

INGREDIENTS

Makes 8–10

140g (4½oz) milk chocolate

240g (2 sticks) unsalted butter

3 eggs

240g (1¼ cups) caster sugar

100g (1 cup) cocoa powder

100g (¾ cup) plain flour

225g (8oz) milk chocolate chips

SPECIAL EQUIPMENT

Mixer or hand-held electric whisk

20 x 30cm (8 x 12in) tin, lined

1 Preheat the oven to 180°C (160°C fan/350°F/Gas 4).

2 Melt the chocolate and butter together until liquid and stir until combined.

3 Mix the eggs and sugar in a mixer (or in a mixing bowl using a hand-held electric whisk). Slowly add the melted chocolate and butter mixture while still mixing on a low speed.

4 Sift in the cocoa powder and flour, and mix again, remembering to scrape down the sides with a spatula.

5 Add 200g (7oz) of the chocolate chips and fold in with a spoon or with the mixer on a low speed.

6 Spoon the mixture into the lined tin and evenly spread it right up to the edges. Scatter with the remaining 25g (1oz) of chocolate chips.

7 Bake in the preheated oven for 30 minutes, or until a toothpick, inserted 5cm (2in) from the edge, comes out clean. The middle should still wobble. Leave to cool completely in the tin.

8 Chill the brownies in the fridge for a couple of hours to achieve a fudgy texture. Cut into squares or rectangles and serve them warm or cold – they're delicious either way!

TOP TIP ★ You can replace the milk chocolate with dark chocolate, if you prefer – or try a mixture of both!

CHOCOLATE CARAMEL BROWNIES

This is our original brownie recipe, oozing with home-made salted caramel sauce and packed full of our favourite chocolates, it's an absolute winner on the comfort food scale.

INGREDIENTS

Makes 8–10

2 packets of Rolos

140g (4½oz) milk chocolate

240g (2 sticks) unsalted butter

3 eggs

240g (1¼ cups) caster sugar

100g (1 cup) cocoa powder

100g (¾ cup) plain flour

225g (8oz) milk chocolate chips

100g (3½oz) caramel chocolates

Salted caramel

100g (½ cup) granulated sugar

30g (2 tbsp) unsalted butter, cubed

60ml (¼ cup) double cream

½ tsp sea salt

SPECIAL EQUIPMENT

Mixer or hand-held electric whisk

20 x 30cm (8 x 12in) tin, lined

Piping bag

1 Put the Rolos into the freezer for a couple of hours until frozen.

2 Make a batch of **SALTED CARAMEL** (see page 21) using the quantities listed here.

3 Follow steps 1–4 of the **CHOCOLATE BROWNIES** recipe on page 151.

4 Fold in 200g (7oz) of the chocolate chips. Spoon half the batter into the lined tin and spread it evenly up to the edges of the tin.

5 Load the salted caramel into a piping bag, snip off the end and pipe vertical lines across the top. Use a knife or skewer to drag the caramel in horizontal lines.

6 Spread the rest of the brownie batter evenly over the top and then push the frozen Rolos randomly into the batter. Scatter the remaining 25g (1oz) of chocolate chips over the top.

7 Bake in the preheated oven for 30 minutes, or until a toothpick, inserted into the brownie 5cm (2in) from the edge, comes out clean. The middle should still wobble. Leave to cool in the tin for 10 minutes, then top with the caramel chocolates. Leave to cool completely in the tin.

8 Chill the brownies in the fridge for a couple of hours to achieve a fudgy texture. Cut into squares or rectangles and serve warm or cold. Save any leftover salted caramel to drizzle over the top of ice cream.

TOP TIP ★ Use bake-stable chocolate chips throughout the brownie mixture to ensure they don't melt whilst in the oven.

CREME EGG BROWNIES

Our original brownie recipe is combined with Cadbury's Creme Eggs to make the ultimate Easter brownie with layers of chocolate chips and that sweet fondant centre of a Creme Egg. You can enjoy this one any time of year!

INGREDIENTS

Makes 8–10

140g (4½oz) milk chocolate

240g (2 sticks) unsalted butter

3 eggs

240g (1¼ cups) caster sugar

100g (1 cup) cocoa powder

100g (¾ cup) plain flour

225g (8oz) milk chocolate chips

Creme Egg filling

2 batches of Creme Egg Filling (see page 22)

Decoration

3 Cadbury's Creme Eggs, halved

SPECIAL EQUIPMENT

Mixer or hand-held electric whisk

20 x 30cm (8 x 12in) tin, lined

2 piping bags

1 Make the **CREME EGG FILLING** (see page 22). This will need to be made in advance due to the chilling of the sugar syrup. Divide the mixture in half and colour one portion orange and leave the rest white. Fill one piping bag with orange filling and one with white.

2 Follow steps 1–4 of the **CHOCOLATE BROWNIES** recipe on page 151.

3 Fold in 200g (7oz) of the chocolate chips. Spoon half the batter into the lined tin and spread it evenly up to the edges of the tin.

4 Snip off the ends of the piping bags and pipe vertical lines onto the batter, alternating between the two colours. Pull a knife or skewer through the filling horizontally and back again, creating a feathered pattern. Pour the rest of the brownie batter over the top and repeat with the rest of the Creme Egg filling.

5 Scatter the remaining 25g (1oz) of milk chocolate chips over the top.

6 Bake in the preheated oven for 30 minutes, or until a toothpick, inserted into the brownie 5cm (2in) from the edge, comes out clean. The middle should still wobble.

7 Leave to cool in the tin for 10 minutes, then add the halved Creme Eggs, cut-side up, to decorate.

8 Leave to cool completely in the tin and then chill for a minimum of 6 hours or overnight before cutting into squares or rectangles.

SLUTTY BROWNIES

This internet sensation comprises layers of cookie, Oreo and brownie... with a twist! Filled with colourful confectionery, this brownie–cookie hybrid not only looks amazing, it is perfect for those who just want both! Use any brightly coloured chocolates you like – Smarties, M&Ms or even Mini Eggs work well.

INGREDIENTS

Makes 8–10

150g (5oz) milk chocolate

180g (1½ sticks) unsalted butter

2 eggs

180g (¾ cup plus 2 tbsp) caster sugar

75g (¾ cup) cocoa powder

75g (⅔ cup) plain flour

165g (5½oz) milk chocolate chips, plus 50g (1¾oz) for the top

220g (8oz) Smarties or M&Ms

50ml (3½ tbsp) boiling water

Cookie layer

135g (1⅛ sticks) unsalted butter, melted

115g (½ cup plus 1 tbsp) granulated sugar

115g (½ cup plus 1 tbsp) light soft brown sugar

1 egg plus 1 egg yolk

225g (1¾ cups) plain flour

¾ tsp baking powder

35g (2½ tbsp) golden syrup

115g (4oz) white chocolate chips

115g (4oz) milk chocolate chips

200g (7oz) Smarties or M&Ms

Biscuit layer

300g (10oz) white chocolate

50ml (3½ tbsp) vegetable oil

100g (⅔ cup) sprinkles

2 packets of Oreos (or 1 packet of Oreos and 1 of Crunch Creams)

SPECIAL EQUIPMENT

Mixer or hand-held electric whisk

20cm (8in) square tin, lined

1 For the cookie layer, follow steps 2–3 of the **CHEWY CHOCOLATE CHIP COOKIES** recipe on page 113, using the quantities listed here and adding the Smarties or M&Ms with the chocolate chips. Press the cookie dough into the bottom of the lined tin.

2 For the biscuit layer, melt the white chocolate and add the vegetable oil to prevent cracking when later cooked. Leave to cool slightly and add the sprinkles. Arrange the Oreos over the cookie base, sitting them side by side. Press them in slightly and pour the white chocolate and sprinkle mix over, pushing it up to the edges of the tin with a spoon. Chill in the fridge until firm.

3 Follow steps 1–4 of the **CHOCOLATE BROWNIES** recipe on page 151, using the quantities listed here.

4 Fold in the chocolate chips and Smarties or M&Ms. Pour the boiling water into the brownie mix and stir until combined.

5 Pour the brownie batter into the tin over the solid white chocolate layer, and spread the mixture up to the edges of the tin. Scatter the extra 50g (1¾oz) of chocolate chips over the top.

6 Bake in the preheated oven for 30 minutes, or until the edges of the brownie are cooked and the middle still wobbles.

7 Leave to cool completely in the tin, then chill in the fridge for a couple of hours before cutting into squares or rectangles.

VEGAN CHOCOLATE CHIP BROWNIES

Whether you're trying to give up animal products completely, cut back, or simply want to see if they're as tasty as the real thing, these egg- and milk-free brownies are for you. Fudgy and dense, they are just as delicious as our non-vegan brownies... who could resist?

INGREDIENTS

Makes 8–10

300ml (1¼ cups) dairy-free milk (soya, almond or oat milk work really well)

1 tbsp apple cider vinegar

1½ tsp baking powder

225g (8oz) dairy-free dark chocolate

150g (¾ cup) caster sugar

150g (¾ cup packed) light soft brown sugar

1½ tsp vanilla extract

100ml (6½ tbsp) vegetable oil

185g (1½ cups) plain flour

75g (¾ cup) cocoa powder

½ tsp salt

200g (7oz) dairy-free dark chocolate chips

SPECIAL EQUIPMENT

Mixer or hand-held electric whisk

20 x 30cm (8 x 12in) tin, lined

TOP TIP ★ A lot of dark chocolate still contains milk, so make sure you are using one with no milk in the ingredients. Alternatively, you can purchase vegan chocolate from specialist shops!

1 Preheat the oven to 180°C (160°C fan/350°F/Gas 4).

2 Put the dairy-free milk, apple cider vinegar and baking powder into the bowl of a mixer (or a mixing bowl if using a hand-held electric whisk) and leave to curdle.

3 Melt the chocolate in a bain marie on the hob or in short bursts in the microwave at full power, making sure to keep stirring until the chocolate has fully melted.

4 Once the milk mixture has curdled, place it in the mixer and, using the whisk attachment, whisk for 3–4 minutes until frothy (alternatively, use a hand-held electric whisk). Add the melted chocolate. Using the paddle attachment (if using a mixer), mix on a low speed.

5 Add the caster sugar, light soft brown sugar, vanilla extract and vegetable oil and continue to mix.

6 Sift the flour and cocoa powder into another bowl. Mix these two dry ingredients together, then add into the wet mixture, along with the salt, and keep mixing on a low speed until combined. Once mixed, add 150g (5oz) of the chocolate chips.

7 Pour the batter into the lined tin and use the back of a spoon to spread it evenly to the edges of the tin. Sprinkle the rest of the chocolate chips on top.

8 Bake in the preheated oven for 30 minutes. The brownies should have a slight wobble once removed from the oven. Allow to cool completely in the tin and then chill in the fridge overnight or for several hours before cutting into squares or rectangles.

LOADED WHITE CHOCOLATE BLONDIES

All of our blondie recipes are packed with white chocolate, but this recipe takes it to the next level! Studded with chocolate chips and all the white chocolate treats we could find, then topped with a thick chocolate layer... this is one of our sweetest, most indulgent recipes.

INGREDIENTS

Makes 8–10

250g (9oz) assorted white chocolate bars, such as White Twix, White Buttons, Kinder, etc

150g (1¼ sticks) unsalted butter

100g (3½oz) white chocolate

100g (½ cup) caster sugar

50g (¼ cup packed) light soft brown sugar

2 eggs plus 1 egg yolk

¼ tsp salt

30g (1½ tbsp) golden syrup

250g (scant 2 cups) plain flour

1 heaped tbsp cornflour

200g (7oz) white chocolate chips

2 tsp vanilla extract

Topping

300g (10oz) white chocolate

25ml (1 tbsp plus 2 tsp) vegetable oil

Assorted white chocolates or white chocolate bars, chopped

SPECIAL EQUIPMENT

Mixer or hand-held electric whisk

20 x 30cm (8 x 12in) tin, lined

Piping bag

1 Cut the assorted white chocolate bars into pieces and freeze them for a couple of hours until completely frozen. This will stop them from melting whilst in the oven.

2 Preheat the oven to 180°C (160°C fan/350°F/Gas 4).

3 Melt the butter and white chocolate together in the microwave at full power or gently on the hob. Stir with a spoon or spatula until combined.

4 Put the caster sugar and light soft brown sugar into the bowl of a mixer, then pour in the melted butter and chocolate mixture. Mix on a medium setting for 1 minute. Alternatively, use a mixing bowl and a hand-held electric whisk.

5 Whisk the eggs and egg yolk together, then add to the mixture with the salt and golden syrup, mixing on a low speed.

6 Sift the plain flour and cornflour together into the bowl, before mixing by hand or on a low speed. When combined, add the white chocolate chips and vanilla extract, and mix gently.

7 Pour half of the mixture into the lined tin and spread evenly up to the edges. Distribute the chopped assorted frozen white chocolate bars over the mixture, then pour the remainder of the batter over the top. Use a spoon to spread the batter evenly right up to the edges. Bake in the preheated oven for 25 minutes until the edges are golden brown and the middle still wobbles.

8 Allow to cool in the tin. Once cold, chill for 6 hours or overnight.

9 Make the topping by gently melting the white chocolate in the microwave at full power or over a bain marie. Mix in the vegetable oil. Pour over the cooled brownie in its tin and spread evenly. Decorate with more white chocolates. Leave to set. Use a sharp knife to cut the blondies into equal pieces.

JAMMIE DODGER BLONDIES

Filled with white chocolate chips, swirled with strawberry jam and topped with Jammie Dodgers, these blondies are our kryptonite! Fudgy and sweet, this recipe will be top of your list to bake for your emergency freezer treat stash!

INGREDIENTS

Makes 8–10

170g (1½ sticks) unsalted butter

100g (3½oz) white chocolate

100g (½ cup) caster sugar

100g (½ cup packed) light soft brown sugar

2 eggs plus 1 egg yolk

¼ tsp salt

30g (1½ tbsp) golden syrup

250g (scant 2 cups) plain flour

1 heaped tbsp cornflour

150g (5oz) white chocolate chips

2 tsp vanilla extract

Topping

150g (5oz) strawberry or raspberry jam

12–15 Mini Jammie Dodgers

50g (1¾oz) white chocolate chips

SPECIAL EQUIPMENT

Mixer or hand-held electric whisk

20 x 30cm (8 x 12in) tin, lined

Piping bag

1 Follow steps 2–5 of the **LOADED WHITE CHOCOLATE BLONDIES** recipe (see page 160), using the quantities listed here.

2 Sift the plain flour and cornflour together into the bowl, before mixing by hand or on a low speed. When combined, add 150g (5oz) of the white chocolate chips and the vanilla extract, and mix gently.

3 Pour the mixture into the lined tin, spreading it evenly right up to the edges of the tin.

4 For the topping, spoon the jam into a piping bag and snip the end off. Pipe 6 lines vertically down the rectangular tin, evenly spaced. Use a knife or skewer to drag the jam back and forth horizontally, creating a feathered pattern.

5 Distribute the Jammie Dodgers and the remaining white chocolate chips evenly across the top of the blondie batter.

6 Bake in the preheated oven for 30 minutes, or until the edges are golden brown and the middle still wobbles.

7 Allow to cool completely in the tin. Once cold, chill in the fridge for at least 6 hours or overnight before cutting into squares or rectangles.

TOP TIP ★ Do not be put off by the wobble once cooked – the blondie will look undercooked until completely set! Allow to cool completely, and then put it in the fridge for several hours before cutting. We like to leave them overnight to make sure they are fully set.

APPLE & CINNAMON BLONDIES

Our cinnamon blondies are swirled with Bramley apples and caramel.
When these are in the oven, they will fill your house with the most amazing smell.

INGREDIENTS

Makes 8–10

170g (1½ sticks) unsalted butter

100g (3½oz) white chocolate

100g (½ cup) caster sugar

100g (½ cup packed) light soft brown sugar

2 eggs plus 1 egg yolk

¼ tsp salt

30g (1½ tbsp) golden syrup

250g (scant 2 cups) plain flour

1 heaped tbsp cornflour

3 heaped tsp ground cinnamon, or to taste

150g (5oz) white chocolate chips

2 tsp vanilla extract

Topping

80g (3oz) caramel (see page 21 or use store-bought caramel sauce)

80g (3oz) Bramley apple sauce

½ tablespoon ground cinnamon

1 tablespoon light soft brown sugar

50g (1¾oz) white chocolate chips

SPECIAL EQUIPMENT

Mixer or hand-held electric whisk

20 x 30cm (8 x 12in) tin, lined

Piping bags

1 Follow steps 2–5 of the **LOADED WHITE CHOCOLATE BLONDIES** recipe (see page 160), using the quantities listed here and adding the ground cinnamon into the batter.

2 Sift the plain flour and cornflour together into the bowl, before mixing by hand or on a low speed. When combined, add 150g (5oz) of the white chocolate chips and the vanilla extract, and mix gently.

3 Pour the mixture into the lined tin, spreading it evenly right up to the edges of the tin.

4 Load one piping bag with caramel sauce and another with Bramley apple sauce, and snip off the tips. Use the piping bags to pipe alternate vertical lines. Use a knife or skewer to drag the caramel and apple sauce back and forth horizontally, creating a feathered pattern.

5 Mix the cinnamon and brown sugar together. Using a tablespoon, sprinkle the cinnamon sugar over the top of the blondie batter until covered. Scatter the remaining white chocolate chips over the top and then bake in the preheated oven for 30 minutes, or until the edges are golden brown and the middle still wobbles.

6 Allow to cool completely in the tin. Once cold, chill in the fridge for 6 hours or overnight before cutting into pieces.

TOP TIPS

★ To save time, you could use jarred caramel from any supermarket.

★ We recommend using bake-stable chocolate chips to prevent melting whilst baking.

★ Use a straight-edge tin rather than an angled one to prevent the blondies from sinking in the middle.

FROSTED UNICORN BLONDIES

An absolute favourite at children's and adult's birthday parties alike – who says unicorns are just for kids anyway?! Light colours swirled together and topped with decorative pastel piping make a big statement for these pretty blondies – with the taste to match.

INGREDIENTS

Makes 8–10

220g (2 sticks) unsalted butter

125g (4oz) white chocolate

125g (⅔ cup) caster sugar

125g (½ cup packed plus 2 tbsp) light soft brown sugar

3 eggs

¼ tsp salt

40g (2 tbsp) golden syrup

285g (2 cups plus 2 tbsp) plain flour

1 heaped tbsp cornflour

2 tsp vanilla extract

Pink, purple and teal gel food colouring (or other colours of choice)

200g (7oz) white chocolate chips

Buttercream

100g (7 tbsp) unsalted butter

200g (1½ cups) icing sugar

Flavouring of choice (optional)

Pink, orange, yellow, green, blue, lilac and purple gel food colouring (or other colours of choice)

Decoration

Sprinkles and edible glitter (optional)

SPECIAL EQUIPMENT

Mixer or hand-held electric whisk

20 x 30cm (8 x 12in) tin, lined

Piping bag and nozzle of choice

1 Follow steps 2–5 of the **LOADED WHITE CHOCOLATE BLONDIES** recipe (see page 160), using the quantities listed here.

2 Sift the plain flour and cornflour together into the bowl, before mixing by hand or on a low speed and adding the vanilla. When combined, divide the batter evenly among three bowls.

3 Use the gel food colouring to colour each bowl of batter a different colour. Add 50g (1¾oz) of the white chocolate chips to each bowl and mix in.

4 Spoon the coloured batters into the lined tin in alternate spoonfuls, evenly spreading the batter up to the edges of the tin. Use a skewer or knife to drag the mixture horizontally, creating a feathered pattern and blending the colours together.

5 Scatter the remaining 50g (1¾oz) white chocolate chips evenly over the top of the blondie batter.

6 Bake in the preheated oven for 25 minutes, or until the edges start to crisp and the middle still wobbles.

7 Allow to cool completely in the tin. Once cold, chill in the fridge for 6 hours or overnight.

8 Make the **PLAIN BUTTERCREAM** (see page 16) using the quantities listed here, adding flavouring, if you like. Divide the buttercream among seven different bowls and colour them using gel food colourings.

9 Load a piping bag with the nozzle of your choice and follow the multi-tone piping method (see page 24) with the seven different colours.

10 Decorate with sprinkles and edible glitter to finish. Cut into squares or rectangles to serve.

LEMON & BLUEBERRY BLONDIES

A fresh, fruity white chocolate blondie filled with blueberries, conserve and curd. Each bite is tangy yet sweet, and tastes just like summer, even in winter!

INGREDIENTS

Makes 8–10

150g (1¼ sticks) unsalted butter

100g (3½oz) white chocolate

100g (½ cup) caster sugar

50g (¼ cup packed) light soft brown sugar

2 eggs plus 1 egg yolk

¼ tsp salt

30g (1½ tbsp) golden syrup

250g (scant 2 cups) plain flour

1 heaped tbsp cornflour

200g (7oz) white chocolate chips

2 tsp lemon extract, or to taste

80g (scant ½ cup) frozen blueberries

1½ tbsp lemon curd

1½ tbsp blueberry conserve

SPECIAL EQUIPMENT

Mixer or hand-held electric whisk

20 x 30cm (8 x 12in) tin, lined

Piping bags

1 Follow steps 2–5 of the **LOADED WHITE CHOCOLATE BLONDIES** recipe (see page 160), using the lemon extract instead of the vanilla extract.

2 Sift the plain flour and cornflour together into the bowl, before mixing by hand or on a low speed. When combined, add 150g (5oz) of the white chocolate chips and the vanilla extract, and mix gently. Fold in the frozen blueberries with a spatula.

3 Spoon the mixture into the lined tin and evenly spread it to the edges of the tin.

4 Load one piping bag with the lemon curd and one piping bag with the blueberry conserve, and snip the tips off. Pipe thin vertical lines across the batter. Use a knife or skewer to drag the curd and conserve back and forth horizontally to create a feathered pattern. Add the remaining 50g (1¾oz) white chocolate chips to the top of the blondie batter.

5 Bake in the preheated oven for 35 minutes, or until the edges of the blondie are slightly browned. The whole thing will wobble and look very under-baked, but remove it from the oven at this point.

6 Leave to cool completely in the tin and chill it in the fridge for 6 hours or overnight before cutting into squares or rectangles.

TOP TIPS

★ The quality of the lemon extract depends on how much you need to use. The better the quality, the less you will need.

★ Use a straight-edge tin rather than an angled one to prevent the blondies from sinking in the middle.

CHOCOLATE ORANGE BLONDIES

Chocolate orange is usually a flavour most people reserve for Christmas, but these mouthwatering blondies will keep your cravings fulfilled all year round. Delicious white chocolate batter with hints of orange tousled through – grate some zest on top for a pop of colour.

INGREDIENTS

Makes 8–10

1 Terry's Chocolate Orange

170g (1½ sticks) unsalted butter

100g (3½oz) white chocolate

100g (½ cup) caster sugar

100g (½ cup packed) light soft brown sugar

2 eggs plus 1 egg yolk

¼ tsp salt

30g (1½ tbsp) golden syrup

250g (scant 2 cups) plain flour

1 heaped tbsp cornflour

200g (7oz) white chocolate chips

2 tsp orange extract (or the juice of 1 orange), or to taste

Grated zest of ½ orange

Topping

8–10 segments of Terry's Chocolate Orange

3 tbsp milk chocolate spread

Grated zest of ½ orange

50g (1¾oz) milk chocolate chips

SPECIAL EQUIPMENT

Mixer or hand-held electric whisk

20 x 30cm (8 x 12in) tin, lined

Piping bag (optional)

1 Freeze the Chocolate Orange for the batter and the Chocolate Orange segments for the topping for 2 hours until completely frozen. This will stop them from melting whilst in the oven.

2 Follow steps 2–6 of the **LOADED WHITE CHOCOLATE BLONDIES** recipe (see page 160), using the quantities listed here and adding in the orange extract and zest.

3 Pour half of the mixture into the lined tin and spread evenly up to the edges of the tin. Distribute the frozen Chocolate Orange segments (for the batter) in equal spaces over the mixture, and then pour the remainder of the batter over the top. Use a spoon to spread the batter evenly up to the edges.

4 For the topping, melt the chocolate spread in the microwave at full power, and spoon it into vertical lines across the top of the blondie batter. You can do this using a piping bag, if you prefer. Use a skewer or knife, carefully drag the batter horizontally creating a feathered pattern, making sure not to move the frozen Chocolate Orange segments underneath. Sprinkle the grated orange zest on top and scatter over the milk chocolate chips.

5 Bake in the preheated oven for 30 minutes, or until the edges are golden brown and the middle still wobbles.

6 Remove from the oven and carefully place the frozen Chocolate Orange segments for the topping into the surface of the blondie, using one segment per blondie. We have used 10 here!

7 Leave to cool completely in the tin, then chill in the fridge for 6 hours or overnight before cutting into squares or rectangles.

TOP TIP ★ The quality of the orange extract will determine how much you need to use. The better the quality, the less you will need. Orange oil can be stronger than the fresh juice of an orange, however if you add some grated zest it will make for a lovely orange taste to complement the oil.

S'MORES BROWNIE PIE

A dessert to impress your guests with, this is a clever twist on our original brownie recipe, sandwiched between a soft biscuit base and gooey marshmallow top – a nod to our American friends, this is the s'mores equivalent to glamping.

INGREDIENTS

Serves 8–12

105g (3½oz) milk chocolate

180g (1½ sticks) unsalted butter

3 eggs

180g (¾ cup plus 2 tbsp) caster sugar

75g (¾ cup) cocoa powder

75g (⅔ cup) plain flour

200g (7oz) milk chocolate chips

100g (2 cups) mini marshmallows

Biscuit base

150g (5oz) digestive biscuits (about 10 biscuits)

60g (½ stick) unsalted butter, melted

Topping

100g (2 cups) mini marshmallows

2 digestive biscuits, crushed

15g (½oz) broken milk chocolate pieces or chocolate chips

2 tsp cinnamon sugar (1½ tsp granulated sugar mixed with ½ tsp ground cinnamon)

SPECIAL EQUIPMENT

Mixer or hand-held electric whisk

20cm (8in) round cake tin, lined

1   Start by making the biscuit base. Crush the biscuits by blitzing in a food processor or putting them into a sandwich bag and bashing with a rolling pin. Stir into the melted butter until all the biscuit crumbs are coated.

2   Spoon into the lined tin and press down evenly right up to the sides of the tin.

3   Follow steps 1–5 of the **CHOCOLATE BROWNIES** recipe (see page 151), using the quantities listed here and including the mini marshmallows.

4   Spread the brownie mixture evenly over the biscuit base in the tin.

5   Bake in the preheated oven for 35 minutes, then remove. For the topping, scatter over the marshmallows, crushed digestive biscuits, broken chocolate pieces or chocolate chips and the cinnamon sugar. Place under a hot grill for 1–2 minutes, or until the marshmallows have browned.

6   Leave to cool completely in the tin, then chill in the fridge for a couple of hours before removing from the tin and cutting.

TOP TIP ★ You can use a 20cm (8in) square tin instead of a round tin for s'mores brownie slabs.

BANOFFEE PIE

A thick biscuit base topped with layers of milk chocolate, caramel, bananas and whipped cream makes the perfect banoffee pie... and this recipe is no exception. A great British dessert for dinner parties and entertaining guests.

INGREDIENTS

Serves 8–12

4½ bananas

255g (1 cup plus 1 tbsp) condensed milk

145g (¾ cup packed) light soft brown sugar

120g (1 stick) unsalted butter

200g (7oz) milk chocolate, melted

1 tbsp vegetable oil

Base

250g (9oz) digestive biscuits (about 17)

130g (1 stick plus 1 tbsp) unsalted butter, melted

3 tbsp chocolate spread

200g (7oz) milk chocolate, melted

1 tbsp vegetable oil

Topping

600ml (2½ cups) double cream

200g (2 scant cups) icing sugar

Sprinkles

Caramel, to drizzle
(see page 21 or use store-bought caramel sauce)

Melted milk chocolate, to drizzle

SPECIAL EQUIPMENT

20cm (8in) round cake tin, lined

1   Start by making the base. Put the digestive biscuits in a food processor and blitz, leaving some fine crumbs and some larger pieces within the mix. Alternatively, you can put the biscuits into a sandwich bag and crush with a rolling pin. Add the melted butter and, with a spoon, mix together until all the biscuits are coated. Add the chocolate spread and mix in. Spoon the mixture into the bottom of the lined tin. Use the back of a spoon to press it down to an even thickness right up to the edges of the tin.

2   Mix together the melted milk chocolate and vegetable oil. Pour onto the biscuit base and spread with a spoon up to the edges. The oil will stop the chocolate from cracking when the pie is cut.

3   Thinly slice 1½ bananas and stand the slices up against the sides of the tin all around. Chill in the fridge until the chocolate sets.

4   Preheat the oven to 200°C (180°C fan/400°F/Gas 6).

5   Put the condensed milk, brown sugar and butter in a pan and melt, stirring continuously. It will start bubbling, but as it heats it will become more viscous.

6   Take the tin out of the fridge. When the caramel has thickened, take the pan off the heat and pour the caramel over the chocolate. Use a spoon to spread it evenly over the chocolate, making sure it goes right up to the sides of the tin.

7   Bake in the oven for 12 minutes, then leave to cool for 15 minutes.

8   Mix the melted chocolate with the vegetable oil and pour over the top of the caramel. Thinly slice 2 more bananas and layer them over the top. Put into the fridge again until set.

9   For the topping, whisk together the double cream and icing sugar until stiff. Spoon the whipped cream over the top of the pie. Thinly slice the final banana and use it to decorate the top, along with sprinkles and drizzles of caramel sauce and melted milk chocolate. Serve immediately.

CINNAMON ROLLS

Is there anything better than the smell of cinnamon floating around your house in the morning? These cinnamon rolls can be prepared the evening before, as the yeast in the cinnamon buns requires time to rise. Topped with a cream cheese frosting, these are a truly indulgent Sunday morning breakfast.

INGREDIENTS

Makes 12

185ml (¾ cup) full-fat milk

7g (¼oz) sachet active dried yeast

85g (6 tbsp) unsalted butter, melted

30g (2½ tbsp) caster sugar

30g (2½ tbsp) light soft brown sugar

1 egg plus 1 egg yolk, beaten

¼ tsp salt

Pinch of ground cinnamon or a few drops of vanilla extract (optional)

425g (3 cups) strong white bread flour, plus extra if needed and for dusting

Filling

120g (1 stick) unsalted butter

180g (1 scant cup packed) dark soft brown sugar

4 tsp ground cinnamon, or to taste

150g (1 cup) sultanas (optional)

Frosting

50g (3½ tbsp) unsalted butter

100g (1 scant cup) icing sugar

75g (2½oz) full-fat cream cheese

Lemon juice or vanilla extract, to taste

SPECIAL EQUIPMENT

Mixer or hand-held electric whisk

Baking tray, lined

1   Heat the milk until warm (not hot), whisk in the dried yeast and leave for 5 minutes. (If you are using instant dried yeast, it can be added directly to the flour. If not sure, add to the warm milk.)

2   Beat together the melted butter, caster sugar, light brown sugar, beaten egg and egg yolk, salt and cinnamon or vanilla extract, if using, in the mixer using the paddle attachment. (Or use a hand-held electric whisk and then knead the dough by hand.)

3   Sift the flour into a bowl. Add to the wet mix and beat. Add the milk and yeast, and mix using the dough hook for 6–7 minutes (or knead by hand for 10 minutes). If it is too sticky, add flour, a tablespoon at a time. Put into an oiled bowl and cover with cling film or a damp tea towel. Leave until doubled in size; 1–2 hours.

4   For the filling, mix the softened butter, sugar and cinnamon.

5   When the dough has risen, punch it down to release the air. Let it sit for 10 minutes, then roll it out on a flour-dusted work surface into a rectangle, 50 x 40cm (20 x 16in). (If it is easier to work with, split the dough into two smaller portions and roll into two 25 x 40cm/10 x 16in rectangles.) Spread the cinnamon filling out in an even layer across the dough. Add the sultanas, if using.

6   Take one long side of the rectangle and carefully roll it up into a sausage. Cut it into 12 rolls, about 4cm (1½in) thick. Arrange the rolls, flat-side down, on the lined tray and cover with cling film or a damp tea towel. Leave for 1–2 hours, or until the dough expands and the rolls are touching. (If the rolls are being baked the following day, cover with cling film and chill overnight. Bring them to room temperature for 30–45 minutes before baking.)

7   Preheat the oven to 190°C (170°C fan/375°F/Gas 5).

8   Bake in the oven for 25 minutes until golden brown around the edges. The rolls should be touching and have joined together.

9   Mix together the frosting ingredients. Spread on the cooled rolls.

NO BAKES

SUMMER FRUITS WHITE CHOCOLATE CHEESECAKE

This is the perfect summer's day cheesecake and is such a versatile recipe – you can swap the fruits to suit your favourite cheesecake flavours such as lemon, blueberry or strawberry, or anything you like!

INGREDIENTS

Serves 8–10

400g (14oz) white chocolate

300g (1¼ cups) double cream

450g (1lb) full-fat cream cheese

100g (½ cup) caster sugar

100g (¾ cup) frozen raspberries (optional)

A dash of lemon juice

Base

300g (10oz) digestive biscuits (about 20 biscuits)

150g (1 stick plus 2 tbsp) unsalted butter

White chocolate ganache

60ml (4 tbsp) double cream

200g (7oz) white chocolate

Strawberry edge

9–10 strawberries, halved lengthways

Decoration

Raspberries, strawberries and blueberries

Freeze-dried raspberries

SPECIAL EQUIPMENT

20cm (8in) loose-bottomed round cake tin, lined

Mixer or hand-held electric whisk

Cake drum (optional)

Piping bag and nozzle of choice

1 Start by making the base. Blitz the biscuits in a food processor, leaving some pieces slightly larger. You can also put the biscuits into a sandwich bag and crush with a rolling pin.

2 Melt the butter and add to the biscuits, stirring until coated. Spoon the mixture evenly into the bottom of the lined tin and use the back of a spoon to press it down evenly right up to the edges of the tin. Place in the fridge to cool.

3 Make the **WHITE CHOCOLATE GANACHE** (see page 19) and spoon onto the base, spreading it evenly up to the edges.

4 Arrange the halved strawberries around the edge of the tin, cut-side outwards. Chill in the fridge until the ganache sets.

5 For the cheesecake, melt the white chocolate and leave to cool (but not set). In a mixer (or using a hand-held electric whisk), whip the cream until very stiff. Set aside. In another bowl, mix the cream cheese and caster sugar together until fluffy.

6 Add the whipped cream to the cheese and sugar, and fold together with a spatula. Slowly add the cooled white chocolate and mix together until just combined. Fold in the frozen raspberries with a spatula, if using. It should be wet yet stiff. Using a metal spoon, fill the tin with the mixture, making sure to press right up to the strawberries but not moving them. Chill in the fridge for at least 4 hours, or overnight.

7 Slowly push the bottom of the tin up and remove the baking parchment. Place it on a plate or stick down with excess filling onto a cake drum, if using. Use a hot knife to smooth around the edges of the cheesecake, being careful with the strawberries.

8 Put any excess filling mixture into a piping bag fitted with your nozzle of choice. Pipe small whips around the edge and decorate with fresh fruit and freeze-dried raspberries.

BATTENBERG CHEESECAKE

A British classic in a checkerboard cheesecake, this dessert is easier to make than it looks and is guaranteed to turn heads. We have used a lot of white chocolate in this recipe to keep the layers sturdy and equal when cut – if you prefer, you can swap it out for 3 teaspoons of powdered gelatine instead.

INGREDIENTS

Serves 12

Base

350g (12oz) digestive biscuits (about 12 biscuits)

170g (1 stick plus 5 tbsp) unsalted butter, melted

60g (2oz) white chocolate

5ml (1 tsp) vegetable oil

50g (1¾oz) marzipan

4 mini Battenbergs, sliced

Cheesecake filling

400g (14oz) white chocolate

300g (1¼ cups) double cream

450g (1lb) full-fat cream cheese

100g (½ cup) caster sugar

Almond extract, to taste (or a dash of lemon juice)

Pink and yellow gel food colouring

Decoration

Flaked almonds

SPECIAL EQUIPMENT

20cm (8in) loose-bottomed round cake tin, lined

Mixer or hand-held electric whisk

Piping bags and nozzle of choice

Cake drum (optional)

1   For the base, blitz the biscuits in a food processor, leaving some fine crumbs and some larger pieces. Coat them in the melted butter and use the back of a spoon to press the mixture down evenly into the lined tin. Place in the fridge to cool.

2   Roll out the marzipan into a thin layer and place a clean 20cm (8in) tin on top of it. Use a knife to cut around the tin to create a perfect circle. Melt the white chocolate with the oil and mix together; spread just enough of this on the chilled biscuit base to stick the marzipan circle on top of it in the tin. Spread the remaining chocolate and oil mix over the marzipan layer.

3   Line the sides of the tin with the mini Battenberg slices – the chocolate mix should help them to stick. Place back in the fridge.

4   For the filling, melt the white chocolate; set aside to cool. Whip the cream in a mixer until stiff; set aside. Beat the cream cheese and caster sugar together until fluffy, then fold in the cream.

5   Slowly mix in the white chocolate until just combined. Add the almond extract or lemon juice, if using. Divide the mixture in half; add pink colouring to one bowl and yellow to the other. If the mixture is wet, chill in the fridge for a couple of minutes to stiffen.

6   Put each coloured filling into a piping bag. Pipe a blob of one colour into the middle of the base. Switch bags and pipe a ring around it; continue piping rings in alternate colours until you reach the edge. Pipe a second layer on top in the same way, but reverse the order of the colours; continue until you just reach the top of the tin. Smooth over lightly with an angled spatula to even the top and create a marbled effect. Chill in the fridge for at least 4 hours or overnight if you can.

7   Carefully push the cheesecake out of the tin and remove the baking parchment. Secure the cheesecake onto a plate or cake drum with a little cheesecake filling. Use a hot palette knife to smooth the edges. Decorate with mini Battenbergs and flaked almonds. Best served chilled. Store in the fridge up to 3 days.

TRIPLE-LAYERED COOKIE DOUGH CHEESECAKE BAR

Indulge yourself with the ultimate cookie-lover's slice! A layer of biscuit base is topped with soft cookie dough and creamy cheesecake. Two of our favourite desserts combined into one – who could resist?

INGREDIENTS

Serves 10

100g (3½oz) milk chocolate chip cookies

250g (9oz) white chocolate

150ml (⅔ cup) double cream

300g (10oz) full-fat cream cheese

50g (¼ cup) caster sugar

A dash of lemon juice

Biscuit base

350g (12oz) milk chocolate chip cookies

150g (1 stick plus 2 tbsp) unsalted butter

170g (6oz) white chocolate

20ml (4 tsp) vegetable oil

Edible cookie dough

½ batch of Edible Cookie Dough (see page 20)

Decoration

Melted white chocolate, for drizzling

Cookie crumbs, for sprinkling

SPECIAL EQUIPMENT

20cm (8in) square cake tin, lined

Mixer or hand-held electric whisk

Cake drum (optional)

Piping bag and nozzle of choice

1   For the base, blitz the cookies in a food processor, leaving some pieces slightly larger. Or put them into a sandwich bag and crush with a rolling pin. Melt the butter and add to the biscuits, stirring until coated. Spoon the mixture evenly into the bottom of the lined tin and use the back of a spoon to press it down evenly right up to the edges of the tin. Chill in the fridge.

2   Melt the white chocolate and add the vegetable oil. Pour the mix onto the biscuit base until just covered and spread evenly up to the edges. The oil will stop the chocolate from cracking when the cheesecake is cut. Place into the fridge until tacky.

3   Roll out the edible cookie dough to an even thickness. Press into the white chocolate on top of the biscuit base right up to the edges of the tin, filling in any gaps until completely covered.

4   For the cheesecake filling, blitz the cookies in a food processor leaving some pieces slightly larger, but mostly to crumbs.

5   Melt the white chocolate and leave to cool (but not set). In a mixer with the whisk attachment (or using a hand-held electric whisk), whip the cream until very stiff. Scrape down the sides with a spatula and mix again. Set aside. Using another bowl, mix the cream cheese, caster sugar and lemon juice until fluffy.

6   Add the whipped cream to the cheese and sugar and fold together with a spatula. Slowly add the cooled white chocolate and the cookie crumbs and mix together until just combined. Using a metal spoon, fill the tin with the cheesecake mixture.

7   Chill for 4 hours, or overnight. Slowly push the bottom of the tin up and remove the parchment. Place on a chopping board.

8   Use a hot knife or cake scraper to smooth around the edges of the cheesecake. Cut into slices, then drizzle with melted white chocolate and scatter with cookie crumbs.

LEMON & GINGER CHEESECAKE

Zesty lemon cheesecake layered over a dark chocolate ganache and a spicy ginger biscuit base, these fabulous flavours are easily combined using this versatile no-bake recipe.

INGREDIENTS

Serves 8–10

400g (14oz) white chocolate

390ml (1⅔ cups) double cream

585g (21oz) full-fat cream cheese

130g (scant ¾ cup) caster sugar

Grated zest of 2 lemons

2 tsp lemon extract

Base

150g (5oz) dark chocolate

75ml (5 tbsp) double cream

300g (10oz) ginger biscuits

150g (1 stick plus 2 tbsp) unsalted butter, melted

Dried lemons

2 lemons, sliced

Granulated sugar, for sprinkling

Decoration

Chocolate Shards (see page 32), made from 200g (7oz) dark chocolate

Stem ginger, crystallized ginger, grated chocolate and lemon zest

SPECIAL EQUIPMENT

20cm (8in) loose-bottomed round cake tin, lined

Mixer or hand-held electric whisk

TOP TIP ★ You can replace the lemon extract with lemon juice for a sharper lemon flavour and add more or less than this recipe states, depending on preferred taste.

1 Prepare the dried lemons for the decoration several hours or days before you make the cheesecake. Preheat the oven to 160°C (140°C fan/325°F/Gas 3). Place the sliced lemons on a baking tray, sprinkle with sugar and bake in the preheated oven for 30 minutes, or until translucent. Leave out to dry on baking parchment and sprinkle with more sugar.

2 For the base, melt the dark chocolate and cream together to make a ganache. Blitz the ginger biscuits in a food processor, leaving some pieces slightly larger. You can also put the biscuits into a sandwich bag and crush with a rolling pin.

3 Add the melted butter to the biscuits, stirring until coated. Press the biscuit mixture evenly into the lined tin with the back of a spoon, making sure it comes right up to the edges of the tin. Pour the dark chocolate ganache over the biscuit base and spread it out with the back of a spoon. Chill in the fridge until set.

4 For the cheesecake, melt the white chocolate and leave to cool (but not set). Using the whisk attachment of your mixer (or a hand-held electric whisk), whip the cream until very stiff. Scrape down the sides of the bowl with a spatula and mix again. Put the cream to the side and, using another bowl, whisk together the cream cheese and caster sugar, until fluffy.

5 Add the whipped cream, lemon zest and lemon extract, and combine by hand with a spatula. Slowly add the cooled white chocolate and combine. Using a metal spoon, spread the mixture onto the base. Chill for 4 hours or overnight.

6 Slowly push the bottom of the tin up and remove the baking parchment. Place the cheesecake on a plate or a cake drum, using a little excess filling to help fix it in place. Use a hot knife or cake scraper to smooth around the edges of the cheesecake.

7 Decorate with the dried lemons. We also added Chocolate Shards (see page 32), stem ginger, crystallized ginger, some pared lemon zest and grated chocolate.

HARD CANDY LOLLIPOPS

These lollipops can be made at home with just a few ingredients, and the recipe is so versatile – just change the flavours, colours and silicone moulds to your liking. You can even create shapes and sails in the same way as tempered chocolate decorations (see page 32) for your celebration cakes!

INGREDIENTS

Makes 6

480g (2½ cups) granulated sugar

160ml (⅔ cup) water

80g (⅓ cup) glucose syrup

Pinch of cream of tartar

3g whitening powder (optional)

Liquid food colouring of choice

A few drops of flavouring of choice (we have used candy floss extract)

SPECIAL EQUIPMENT

Heat-resistant gloves

Pastry brush

Sugar thermometer

Lollipop moulds or silicone chocolate moulds

1   Put on heat-resistant gloves. Place the granulated sugar, water and glucose syrup into a heavy-based saucepan over a high heat. Stir and bring to the boil. Do not stir after this point.

2   Sugar crystals may be left around the sides of the pan, so, to prevent burning, wash them down the side of the pan using a wet pastry brush.

3   Continue to boil the syrup without stirring until a sugar thermometer reaches 148–150°C (298–302°F). This is the "hard crack" stage, used when making hard-boiled sweets or candy. This temperature may take a while to reach, however, once it is close, it occurs very quickly, which makes burning very easy. Remove from the heat as soon as the thermometer hits this temperature – the liquid should still be clear and transparent; if it is yellowing it has overheated.

4   Add the cream of tartar, whitening powder (if using), liquid food colouring and a few drops of flavouring. Stir until incorporated. Be careful as the boiling syrup may splutter.

5   Carefully pour into moulds and wait until completely cold and set. If using lollipop moulds, make sure that the lollipop stick is already in the mould when the syrup is poured in or is pressed in immediately afterwards. Once cold and set, remove from the moulds.

TOP TIPS

★ Molten sugar is extremely dangerous – it's essential to wear heat-resistant gloves for this recipe, as it can burn you very easily. We also don't recommend making this recipe with children.

★ These lollipops will be transparent whether plain or coloured. Using whitening powder will turn the transparent syrup white; if you are adding colour after this, the lollipops will be opaque.

★ Try flavours like candy floss, strawberry and bubblegum!

MILK CHOCOLATE ROCKY ROAD

Our milk chocolate rocky road can be cut into squares and towered up high to make a fantastic (and quick!) alternative to a layer cake. Easy to make, and so tasty, we've got you covered for any of those forgotten birthdays – just stick some candles in and all will be forgiven.

INGREDIENTS

Makes 8–10

400g (14oz) digestive biscuits (about 26 biscuits)

100g (2 cups) mini marshmallows

50g (1¾oz) milk chocolate chips

275g (9½oz) mixed milk chocolate bars of your choice

130g (1 stick plus 1 tbsp) unsalted butter

350g (12oz) milk chocolate

125g (½ cup) golden syrup

Topping

400g (14oz) milk chocolate

30ml (2 tbsp) vegetable oil

25g (¼ cup) mini marshmallows

Milk chocolate bars of your choice, to decorate

Sprinkles

SPECIAL EQUIPMENT

20 x 30cm (8 x 12in) tin, lined

1 Crush the biscuits by blitzing in a food processor or putting them into a sandwich bag and bashing with a rolling pin, making sure to leave some smaller and larger pieces. Tip into a bowl.

2 Add the mini marshmallows, chocolate chips and the milk chocolate bars (we used chocolate buttons, crispy M&Ms, Smarties and Terry's Chocolate Orange segments). Stir the dry ingredients together.

3 Melt together the unsalted butter, milk chocolate and golden syrup until liquid and combined.

4 Pour the wet ingredients into the dry ingredients and stir until completely coated.

5 Spoon the rocky road into the lined tin and press down in an even layer with the back of a spoon.

6 For the topping, melt the milk chocolate and stir in the vegetable oil. Scatter the marshmallows over the top of the rocky road and pour the melted chocolate over. Use a spoon to gently spread it evenly up to the edges of the tin.

7 Decorate with more milk chocolate bars and sprinkles. Set at room temperature overnight, or place in the fridge to speed up the process. Use a sharp knife to cut into squares or rectangles. Biscuits can go soft quickly, however, rocky road should stay fresh for up to a week if wrapped with cling film or foil.

WHITE CHOCOLATE ROCKY ROAD

A blend of biscuits, white chocolate, marshmallows and syrup, this much sought-after rocky road causes queues outside our shop, and now the recipe is yours to enjoy.

INGREDIENTS

Makes 8–10

400g (14oz) digestive biscuits (about 26 biscuits)

100g (2 cups) mini marshmallows

50g (1¾oz) white chocolate chips

275g (9½oz) mixed white chocolate bars of your choice

120g (1 stick) unsalted butter

350g (12oz) white chocolate

125g (½ cup) golden syrup

Topping

400g (14oz) white chocolate

30ml (2 tbsp) vegetable oil

25g (¼ cup) mini marshmallows

Mixed white chocolate bars of your choice, to decorate

Sprinkles

Edible glitter

SPECIAL EQUIPMENT

20 x 30cm (8 x 12in) tin, lined

1   Crush the biscuits by blitzing in a food processor or putting them into a sandwich bag and bashing with a rolling pin, making sure to leave some smaller and larger pieces. Tip into a bowl.

2   Add the mini marshmallows, white chocolate chips and white chocolate bars (we used white Twix, Bueno, white chocolate buttons and chopped up white chocolate). Stir the dry ingredients together.

3   Melt together the unsalted butter, white chocolate and golden syrup until liquid and combined.

4   Pour the wet ingredients into the dry ingredients and stir until completely coated.

5   Spoon the rocky road into the lined tin and press down evenly with the back of a spoon.

6   For the topping, melt the white chocolate and stir in the vegetable oil. Scatter the marshmallows over the top of the rocky road and pour the melted chocolate over. Use a spoon to spread it evenly up to the edges of the tin.

7   Decorate the top with more white chocolate bars, sprinkles and edible glitter. Set at room temperature overnight, or place in the fridge to speed up the process. Use a sharp knife to cut into squares or rectangles. Biscuits can go soft quickly, however, rocky road should stay fresh for up to a week if wrapped with cling film or foil.

TOP TIP ★ We recommend using bake-stable chocolate chips to prevent them from melting within the mix.

SALTED CARAMEL ROCKY ROAD

Just when you think our rocky road couldn't get any better, throw in some salted caramel and salty snacks to make the perfectly salty-sweet no-bake dessert. It's easy to make, but the downside is that, unfortunately, you do have to wait a few hours for it to set before you can enjoy a slice!

INGREDIENTS

Makes 8–10

300g (10oz) digestive biscuits (about 16)

75g (2½oz) mini salted pretzels

50g (1¾oz) chocolate caramel wafer bars

125g (2½ cups) mini marshmallows

50g (1¾oz) white chocolate chips

150g (5oz) mixed caramel chocolate bars of your choice

130g (1 stick) unsalted butter

250g (9oz) white chocolate

100g (6½ tbsp) golden syrup

Salted caramel

200g (1 cup) granulated sugar

60g (½ stick) unsalted butter, cubed

120ml (½ cup) double cream

½ tsp sea salt

Topping

400g (14oz) milk chocolate

30ml (2 tbsp) vegetable oil

Caramel chocolates, mini salted pretzels, sprinkles and edible glitter

SPECIAL EQUIPMENT

20 x 30cm (8 x 12in) tin, lined

1 Make the **SALTED CARAMEL** (see method on page 21) using the quantities listed here. This can be made and stored weeks before making the rocky road.

2 Crush the digestive biscuits and pretzels together by blitzing in a food processor or adding to a sandwich bag and bashing with a rolling pin, making sure to leave some smaller and larger pieces. Chop up the chocolate caramel wafer bars and add to a bowl with the crushed biscuits and pretzels.

3 Add 100g (2 cups) of the mini marshmallows, the white chocolate chips and caramel chocolate bars (we used Dairy Milk with caramel, caramel buttons and Twix). Stir the dry ingredients together.

4 Melt the unsalted butter, white chocolate, golden syrup and half the salted caramel together until liquid. Pour the wet ingredients into the dry ingredients and stir until completely coated.

5 Spoon the rocky road into the lined tin and press down evenly with the back of a spoon. For the topping, melt the milk chocolate and stir in the vegetable oil. Scatter the remaining 25g (½ cup) of marshmallows over the top of the rocky road and pour the melted chocolate over. Use a spoon to gently spread it evenly up to the edges of the tin.

6 Use the rest of the salted caramel to drizzle lines over the top of the chocolate. Drag a skewer or knife gently back and forth to create a feathered pattern.

7 Decorate with more caramel chocolates, pretzels, sprinkles and edible glitter. Set at room temperature overnight, or place in the fridge to speed up the process. Use a sharp knife to cut into squares or rectangles. Biscuits can go soft quickly, however, rocky road should stay fresh for up to a week if wrapped with cling film or foil.

LOTUS BISCOFF ROCKY ROAD

A blend of biscuits, chocolate, marshmallows and syrup, this recipe combines our much sought-after rocky road and the delicious flavour of Lotus Biscoff.

INGREDIENTS

Makes 8–10

500g (18oz) Lotus Biscoff biscuits

200g (7oz) digestives (about 14)

125g (1 stick) unsalted butter

175g (¾ cup) golden syrup

220g (4⅓ cups) mini marshmallows

200g (7oz) white chocolate

75g (⅓ cup) Lotus Biscoff spread

Topping

250g (9oz) white chocolate

100g (⅓ cup plus 2 tbsp) Lotus Biscoff spread

Decoration

20g (¾oz) crushed Lotus Biscoff biscuits

20g (¾oz) white chocolate curls

8–10 Lotus Biscoff biscuits

SPECIAL EQUIPMENT

20 x 30cm (8 x 12in) tin, lined

1   Put 400g (14oz) of the Lotus Biscoff biscuits and all the digestive biscuits in a food processor and blitz, leaving some fine crumbs and some larger pieces. Alternatively, you can put the biscuits into a sandwich bag and crush with a rolling pin. Once crushed, transfer them to a pan with the butter, 125g (½ cup) of the syrup and 100g (2 cups) of the marshmallows, and melt until combined over a gentle heat. Transfer the mixture into a heatproof bowl.

2   Melt the white chocolate with the Lotus Biscoff spread (either in a microwave at full power in 20-second bursts, or in a bain marie). Mix until the chocolate is a beige colour and add into the biscuit mix. Mix together until completely coated and leave to cool for 5 minutes.

3   Blitz the remaining Lotus Biscoff biscuits and stir them into the mix.

4   After 5 minutes, add a further 100g (2 cups) of marshmallows and the remaining 50g (3 tbsp) of golden syrup into the bowl and combine until evenly distributed. The mixture should be cool enough not to melt the marshmallows.

5   Press the rocky road mixture into the lined tin, evenly and right up to the edges of the tin. Scatter the remaining 20g (⅓ cup) of marshmallows over the top.

6   For the topping, melt the white chocolate and Lotus Biscoff spread together, and stir. Pour over the top of the rocky road and spread evenly until covered.

7   Decorate with the crushed Lotus Biscoff biscuits, white chocolate curls and the whole Lotus Biscoff biscuits. Set at room temperature overnight, or place in the fridge to speed up the process. Use a sharp knife to cut into squares or rectangles. Biscuits can go soft quickly, however, rocky road should stay fresh for up to a week if wrapped with cling film or foil.

HOT CHOCOLATE BOMBS

Hot chocolate bombs are the latest craze. Fill these chocolate spheres with hot chocolate powder and mini marshmallows, put into a mug and pour steaming milk over the top. Enjoy your favourite hot chocolate with a luxury twist.

INGREDIENTS

Makes 6

300g (10oz) white or milk chocolate, plus an extra 50g (1¾oz)

20ml (4 tsp) vegetable oil

6 portions of hot chocolate powder (follow the quantities on the tub)

About 6 tbsp mini marshmallows

Chocolates of choice, for decorating (optional)

Oil-based food colouring (optional)

SPECIAL EQUIPMENT

12-hole half-sphere silicone chocolate mould *(available from our website)*

Large muffin cases (optional)

TOP TIPS

★ Add a tablespoon of Lotus Biscoff spread or Nutella spread into the melted chocolate to create a flavoured hot chocolate.

★ Use oil-based food colouring to create different colour bombs.

1 Melt the 300g (10oz) of chocolate and add the vegetable oil. The oil adds shine to the bombs, but if you prefer, you can temper the chocolate (see page 30).

2 Spoon a little melted chocolate into each mould and, either using the back of the spoon or a pastry brush, wipe the chocolate up the sides of the mould, right up to the top. Tip the mould upside-down over the chocolate bowl so the excess drips back into the bowl – this will prevent the chocolate from pooling. If the chocolate is too thick in places, it will be difficult to add the mini marshmallows and hot chocolate powder without them escaping. Using a cake scraper or a knife, scrape over the top of the mould to remove the excess chocolate. Freeze the moulds for a couple of minutes before taking them back out and repeating, adding another layer of melted chocolate.

3 After they have set, gently pop the chocolate spheres out by turning the moulds over and carefully peeling away the silicone. This will stop the delicate edges from breaking.

4 The two halves of the sphere then need to be stuck together; you can do so on a slightly warmed pan or use a warm knife or metal cake scraper (these can be put in hot water for a few seconds and dried to heat them). Hold both sides of the half-spheres and gently place both on the warm metal for a second, then work quickly to fill one shell with the spoonful of hot chocolate powder and mini marshmallows. Quickly sandwich them together whilst still slightly melted (we wear disposable vinyl gloves during this process), and then wipe the excess melted chocolate around the sphere with your finger.

5 Add a small blob of melted chocolate into the bottom of each large muffin case and carefully put a sphere inside.

6 We decorated these spheres with more melted chocolate, freeze-dried raspberry pieces, chocolate curls, edible glitter and used food colouring, but with these, anything goes. Put one in a mug, pour boiling milk over the top and watch the magic!

PEANUT BUTTER CUPS

A play on the famous peanut butter cups, these extra-large, deep-filled, crunchy yet sweet cups are so quick to make it'll be hard not to eat them all!

INGREDIENTS

Makes 6

325g (11oz) milk chocolate

50g (3½ tbsp) unsalted butter

150g (⅔ cup) smooth peanut butter

50g (1¾oz) digestive biscuits, crushed (about 3½ biscuits)

100g (¾ cup) icing sugar

Pinch of salt

SPECIAL EQUIPMENT

12-hole cupcake tin, lined with 6 cases

1   Temper the milk chocolate (see page 30). Carefully spoon a little mixture into the bottom of six cupcake cases. Leave to set. Save the remaining chocolate for later.

2   Melt the unsalted butter and peanut butter together and stir. Add the crushed digestive biscuits and stir until coated. Gradually add the icing sugar and combine everything together with a spoon until a paste forms. Add the salt and leave to cool for 5 minutes.

3   Once the chocolate layer has set, gently pack the peanut butter mixture evenly into the chocolate cases, pushing it down in an even layer with the back of a spoon.

4   Re-melt the remaining chocolate and pour over the peanut butter mixture, creating a top layer, then put in the fridge to set.

5   Peel away the paper cases to serve.

CHOCOLATE GANACHE BALLS

These really are mouthfuls of heaven! Creamy ganache encased in a hard shell of chocolate, these are perfect for a dessert table, or to create an extra-special finish piled on top of a celebration cake or cheesecake. Add oil-based food colouring to white chocolate, if you like.

INGREDIENTS

Makes 6

300g (10oz) white or milk chocolate, plus an extra 50g (1¾oz) for decorating

Chocolates and sprinkles, for decorating (optional)

White chocolate ganache

150g (⅔ cup) double cream

300g (10oz) white chocolate

SPECIAL EQUIPMENT

Mixer or hand-held electric whisk

12-hole half-sphere silicone chocolate mould
(available from our website)

Piping bag

6 large muffin cases (optional)

1   First make a batch of **WHITE CHOCOLATE GANACHE** (see page 19) with the quantities listed here, and leave to set. (Ideally, leave at room temperature and use the same day, however, you can put it in the fridge to speed up the process or to use another day.) Transfer the mixture to the mixer bowl. When the ganache has cooled down, it will create a thick rubbery skin as the chocolate and cream start to set.

2   Temper the chocolate following the instructions on page 30, then follow steps 2–3 of the **HOT CHOCOLATE BOMBS** (see page 198) to create the chocolate spheres.

3   Once the ganache has started to harden slightly, use the whisk attachment of the mixer (or a hand-held electric whisk) to whip the ganache for around 5 minutes. If the texture is quite wet, put the mixture into the fridge for 15 minutes, then whip again. The texture of the ganache should be like thick whipping cream and should scrape around the bowl easily. If the ganache has set too hard, try leaving it at room temperature for 30 minutes or add a splash of extra cream to loosen it.

4   Load the ganache into a piping bag and snip the end off. Melt the extra 50g (1¾oz) of chocolate and set aside.

5   The two halves of the sphere then need to be stuck together; you can do so on a slightly warmed pan or using a warm knife or metal cake scraper (these can be put under hot water for a few seconds and dried to heat them). Hold both sides of the half-spheres and gently place both on the warm metal for a second, then work quickly to fill with the ganache. Quickly sandwich them together whilst still slightly melted (we wear disposable vinyl gloves during this process) and then wipe the excess melted chocolate around the sphere with your finger.

6   Add a blob of the melted chocolate into the bottom of each large muffin case and carefully put the spheres inside. Drizzle over the remaining melted chocolate to decorate. We added chocolate curls, sprinkles and a piece of chocolate to the tops.

GEO-HEART CAKE SHAPES

These make for impressive little favours for weddings and baby showers, and even for adorning a cake. There are plenty of different moulds available to make all kinds of intricate shapes – we've chosen geometric hearts as they are one of the most popular. Quantities may change depending on your mould design.

INGREDIENTS

Makes 12 geometric hearts

375g (13oz) any cake

75g (2½oz) your chosen buttercream (see pages 16–17)

300–400g (10–14oz) chocolate of choice

Oil-based food colouring (optional)

Decorations (such as edible silver and gold leaf, sprinkles, dried fruit pieces and edible glitter)

SPECIAL EQUIPMENT

Silicone geometric heart mould *(available from our website)*

TOP TIP ★ If you are making cake and buttercream specifically for this recipe rather than using leftovers, it's easier to work from a cupcake recipe. You'll need to make about 6 cupcakes and 75g (2½oz) buttercream made from 25g (2 tbsp) butter and 50g (⅓ cup) icing sugar (see pages 16–17 for method). Allow the cake to cool completely before using or it will melt the buttercream.

1 Crumble the cake into a mixer bowl and add a small amount of the buttercream. Turn on your mixer to a slow speed (or use a hand-held electric whisk) and beat together, adding more buttercream until the mixture looks smoothly combined, and is moist but not wet. If the texture is too wet, you will need to add more cake. Set aside.

2 Temper the chocolate (see page 30). Add oil-based food colouring, if using.

3 Using a paintbrush or the back of a spoon, evenly coat the inside of each mould with the tempered chocolate, making sure all corners are filled. Turn the mould upside-down and let any excess chocolate drip out. Place the mould into the fridge or freezer for a few minutes until solidified.

4 Once chilled, use a sharp knife to trim away any excess hardened chocolate spilling onto the side of the mould.

5 Weigh out balls of the cake mix to 45g (1½oz) each. Using your hands, push a ball of mix into each mould, making sure that it lies flat rather than domed out of the mould.

6 Spread a small amount of tempered chocolate over the top to seal the shape. Place back in the fridge for 45–60 minutes, or in the freezer to speed up the process.

7 Once solidified, remove the shapes from the silicone mould – they should pop out quite easily. Trim away any excess chocolate with a sharp knife or a pair of scissors and place on a piece of baking parchment to decorate as you wish.

CAKE POPS & CAKESICLES

Cake pops are a really fun and easy way to use up leftover cake and buttercream. Gone are the days of the original cake pop on a stick; now there are silicone moulds that help you achieve all sorts of impressive styles – we love the mini ice cream shapes to make cakesicles. These are perfect little favours and look amazing on a cake, too!

INGREDIENTS

Makes 18 cake pops or 10 cakesicles

375g (13oz) any cake

75g (2½oz) your chosen buttercream (see pages 16–17)

300–400g (10–14oz) chocolate of choice

Oil-based food colourings (optional)

Decorations (such as sprinkles, edible silver and gold leaf, dried fruit pieces and edible glitter)

SPECIAL EQUIPMENT

Baking tray, lined

18 cake pop sticks (for cake pops)

Cake pop stand (or make your own from Styrofoam or a cardboard box)

Silicone mini ice cream mould (for cakesicles)

10 wooden lollipop sticks (for cakesicles)

To make the cake mix

Crumble the cake into a mixer bowl and add a small amount of the buttercream. Turn on your mixer to a slow speed (or use a hand-held electric whisk) and beat together, adding more buttercream until the mixture looks smoothly combined, and is moist but not wet. If the texture is too wet, you will need to add more cake.

Cake pops

1 Weigh out 25g (1oz) batches of the cake mix and roll each into a small ball between your palms. Place the balls on a lined baking tray and refrigerate for 1–2 hours or put in the freezer for 45–60 minutes. Once chilled, roll them again in your palms to get a smoother shape.

2 Temper the chocolate (see page 30) and add an oil-based food colouring, if using. Pour the chocolate into a mug or tall narrow container to be able to fully dip the cake pops.

3 Dip one end of the cake pop sticks into the chocolate, then push this side into your cake pops (this gives the cake pops more strength). Return the tray to the fridge/freezer to help these set.

4 Once chilled, dip each cake pop fully into the chocolate and twist whilst removing. The chocolate should solidify quite quickly around the chilled cake pops. Turn them the correct way up and put them into a cake pop stand to set.

5 Decorate with more melted chocolate, sprinkles or anything you like! ▶

Rainbow cake pops

1   Split the cake mix into 7 portions. Add a small amount of each food colouring to each portion – red, orange, yellow, green, blue, indigo and violet, or any colour combination of your choice. Knead the cake mix until the colours have fully dispersed.

2   Pinch small amounts of each colour into your hand, building them on top of each other until you have enough for one cake pop. Flatten the pile slightly and roll lightly into a ball, combining the colours. Place the balls on a lined baking tray and refrigerate for 1–2 hours or freeze for 45–60 minutes. Once chilled, roll them again in your palms to get a smoother shape.

3   Continue with steps 2–5 of the regular cake pops (see page 205).

Cakesicles

1   Weigh out balls of cake pop mix to 35g (1¼oz). Using your hands, push the mixture into the silicone mould. Secure in the wooden sticks and refrigerate for 2 hours, or freeze for 45–60 minutes.

2   Once chilled, remove the cakesicles from the mould, being careful not to pull the sticks out. Each mould may be different.

3   Temper the chocolate (see page 30) and add oil-based food colouring, if using. Pour the chocolate into a mug or tall narrow container to be able to fully dip the cakesicles.

4   Dip each cakesicle fully into the chocolate and, whilst removing it, wipe the back of the cakesicle against the edge of the mug to remove excess chocolate and prevent spilling. You may want to double-coat the cakesicles in chocolate once the first layer has dried.

5   Place the cakesicles on a piece of baking parchment and decorate to your liking.

SMALL
BAKES

CLASSIC SCONES

Perfect for afternoon tea, this classic scone recipe is delicious with jam and clotted cream.
Enjoy them as they are, or add sultanas, cherries or raspberries to make a deliciously fruity treat.
Our scones are made with rich double cream as well as milk, giving a fluffy and light texture on the
inside and a buttery crust on the outside. Scones are best enjoyed on the day that they are baked.

INGREDIENTS

Makes 8

400g (3¼ cups) self-raising flour,
plus extra for dusting

⅛ tsp salt

1 tsp baking powder

100g (6½ tbsp) unsalted butter,
frozen

55g (½ cup) caster sugar

Up to 100g (3½oz) fruit (optional;
sultanas, glacé cherries or frozen
raspberries work well)

100ml (6½ tbsp) milk, plus an
extra 30ml (2 tbsp)

50ml (3½ tbsp) double cream

A squeeze of lemon juice

A dash of vanilla extract

Beaten egg, for brushing

Icing sugar, for dusting (optional)

Jam and clotted cream, to serve

SPECIAL EQUIPMENT

7cm (3in) pastry cutter
Baking tray, lined

1 Preheat the oven to 220°C (200°C fan/425°F/Gas 7).

2 Sift the self-raising flour, salt and baking powder together into
a bowl. Grate the frozen butter into the dry ingredients and rub
together between your fingertips to form breadcrumbs.

3 Add the caster sugar and fruit (if using) to the crumb mixture
and mix together. Gradually add the milk, double cream,
lemon juice and vanilla extract, and mix by hand until a dough
is formed.

4 Pat the dough together lightly for as little time as possible,
adding the extra 30ml (2 tbsp) of milk as you pat it together. The
dough should be flaky. Add a dusting of flour if it is too sticky.

5 Roll out the dough on a lightly floured surface using a rolling pin
to 2.5cm (1in) thick.

6 Press downwards through the dough with a pastry cutter, being
careful not to twist the cutter, so that the scones cut evenly.
Arrange the scones on a lined baking tray.

7 Brush the scones with beaten egg using a pastry brush.

8 Bake in the preheated oven for 15 minutes, or until they have
started to turn golden brown and risen evenly.

9 Transfer to a wire rack to cool, finish with a dusting of icing sugar
(optional) and serve with jam and clotted cream – essential!

> **TOP TIPS** ★ If you don't have a pastry cutter, use the rim of a glass, or roll
> the scones into ball shapes. They may rise slightly unevenly, but will still be
> equally as delicious. ★ If using fruit, frozen or fresh can be used, but you
> may develop a preference. Frozen fruit prevents sinking, however, it does
> add excess water to the mixture, which can mean the colour from the fruit
> can bleed into the dough. Fresh fruit can start to disintegrate under heat.

LEMON & BLUEBERRY SCONES

Our classic scone recipe packed with zesty lemon and juicy blueberries, giving the perfect balance between sharp and sweet. Top with blueberry conserve or lemon curd and clotted cream to serve.

INGREDIENTS

Makes 6

400g (3¼ cups) self-raising flour, plus extra for dusting

⅛ tsp salt

1 tsp baking powder

100g (6½ tbsp) unsalted butter, frozen

55g (½ cup) caster sugar

100ml (6½ tbsp) milk, plus an extra 30ml (2 tbsp)

50ml (3½ tbsp) double cream

A squeeze of lemon juice

A dash of lemon extract or a little extra lemon juice

Grated zest of 1 lemon, or to taste, plus extra to serve

Up to 100g (3½oz) blueberries, plus extra to serve

Beaten egg, for brushing

Blueberry conserve or lemon curd and clotted cream, to serve

SPECIAL EQUIPMENT

10cm (4in) pastry cutter

Baking tray, lined

1   Follow steps 1–3 of the **CLASSIC SCONES** recipe (see page 211) using the quantities listed here, adding in the lemon extract or extra lemon juice and some grated zest to taste.

2   Pat the dough together lightly for as little time as possible, adding the extra 30ml (2 tbsp) of milk as you pat it together. The dough should be flaky. Add a dusting of flour if it is too sticky. While patting, fold in the blueberries.

3   Roll out the dough using a rolling pin until it is 2.5cm (1in) thick, making sure the blueberries are dotted throughout the dough.

4   Press downwards through the dough with a pastry cutter, being careful not to twist the cutter, so that the scones cut evenly. Arrange the scones on a lined baking tray.

5   Brush the scones with beaten egg using a pastry brush.

6   Bake in the preheated oven for 15 minutes, or until they have started to turn golden brown and risen evenly.

7   Serve with blueberry conserve or lemon curd and clotted cream. Or try it with all three! We also added some extra fresh blueberries and some grated lemon zest.

CINNAMON ROLL SCONES

An alternative to using a yeast dough, we have combined our Cinnamon Rolls (page 176) and Classic Scones (page 211) for this delicious combination, perfect if you are wanting to make the taste of cinnamon rolls but in quick time!

INGREDIENTS

Makes 9–12

400g (3¼ cups) self-raising flour, plus extra for dusting

⅛ tsp salt

1 tsp baking powder

100g (6½ tbsp) unsalted butter, frozen

55g (½ cup) caster sugar

100ml (6½ tbsp) milk, plus an extra 30ml (2 tbsp)

50ml (3½ tbsp) double cream

A squeeze of lemon juice

Beaten egg, for brushing

Filling

120g (1 stick) unsalted butter

180g (1 scant cup packed) dark soft brown sugar

4 tsp ground cinnamon, or to taste

A handful of sultanas (optional)

Frosting (optional)

50g (3½ tbsp) unsalted butter

100g (1 scant cup) icing sugar

75g (2½oz) full-fat cream cheese

Lemon juice or vanilla extract, to taste

SPECIAL EQUIPMENT

Baking tray, lined

1   Follow steps 1–4 of the **CLASSIC SCONES** recipe (see page 211) using the quantities listed here.

2   Make the filling by mixing together the softened butter, dark soft brown sugar and cinnamon. This paste will be the inside of your cinnamon roll.

3   Roll the scone dough out on a flour-dusted work surface into a rectangular shape about 1cm (½in) thick. (If it is easier to work with, split the dough into two smaller amounts.) Spread the cinnamon filling out in an even layer across the rolled-out dough. Sprinkle over a handful of sultanas, if you like.

4   Starting at the longest side of the rectangle, carefully roll up the dough so that it resembles a sausage. Cut it into 9–12 slices.

5   Arrange the scones, flat-side down, on a lined baking tray. Brush the scones with a little bit of beaten egg using a pastry brush.

6   Bake in the preheated oven for about 10–12 minutes, or until golden brown.

7   They can be served plain, or frosting can be added. To make the frosting, beat together the butter, icing sugar and cream cheese. Depending on your preference, flavour with lemon juice or vanilla extract to taste. Make sure the rolls are cooled slightly, then spread on the frosting and serve.

BASIC MACARON SHELLS

A macaron is a beautiful meringue-based cookie sandwich, glued together with buttercream or ganache. The inside is fluffy and the outside crisp and slightly chewy, a combination hard to master and even harder to resist! Use our basic French macaron shell recipe and method and adapt it with any colouring, flavour and filling.

INGREDIENTS

Makes 40 shells

150g (1¼ cups) icing sugar

140g (1⅓ cups) almond flour

90g (⅓ cup plus 1 tbsp) egg whites, at room temperature

¼ tsp cream of tartar

Pinch of salt

80g (6½ tbsp) caster sugar

Gel or powdered food colouring

SPECIAL EQUIPMENT

Mixer or hand-held electric whisk

Piping bag and Stuart #R18L nozzle (or any open round nozzle)

Macaron mat (see page 10)

1   Blitz the icing sugar and almond flour in a food processor to combine, then sieve. Please note, this is not a quick process; it takes us at least 15 minutes to fully strain the powder. We use the back of a spoon to mix and drag the powder through a sieve. This is important for smooth macaron tops, so do persevere! If you are left with stubborn almond pieces, discard them.

2   Using a clean metal bowl (do not use a plastic bowl; metal bowls can be cleaned with vinegar and water to get rid of any hidden grease), whisk the egg whites in a mixer or using a hand-held electric whisk. Whisk on a medium speed until foamy.

3   Add the cream of tartar and whisk on medium speed until soft peaks form.

4   Add the salt. Turn up the speed to high and slowly spoon the caster sugar in, one spoonful every 20 seconds. The mixture should double in size.

5   When you have added all the sugar, turn up the speed to maximum and whisk until it is thick and glossy, stiff peaks form and all the sugar has dissolved. You can check this by rubbing some mixture between your fingers to check for sugar grains. You should be able to hold the bowlful of mixture upside-down without any sliding, and it should feel and look like thick melted marshmallow under your spatula.

6   Add any gel food colouring. Do not use an oil-based colouring as this will deflate the whole mix.

7   The next stage is called macaronage (a French term that means the way dry ingredients and meringue are combined). Add one-third of the icing sugar and almond flour to the meringue and gently fold in, using a figure of 8 action. This starts to knock the air out of the mixture. ▶

TOP TIPS

★ Macarons are quite hard to perfect, from the stiffness of the meringue and the number of folds it takes to make the ideal batter, to your piping technique and the perfect temperature for your oven! Buy an oven thermometer to check the exact temperature your oven is at. And, most importantly, don't give up!

★ You can buy fresh egg whites from some supermarkets if you're uncertain about separating eggs properly. Make sure not to get any egg yolk or grease in the mix as this can compromise the recipe.

8 When combined, add another third. Repeat the folding process.

9 Add the final third and start folding again. The mixture may look and feel very thick and dry, but will soon loosen. Count your strokes – we find around 30–40 will create the perfect batter. Make sure any powder that may be on the bottom of your bowl is combined with the mix. Drag the spatula up the sides of the bowl, wiping the mixture up the bowl and scrape back round the bowl again. You should be able to hear the air bubbles popping. If you hold the spatula over the bowl, the mixture should flow back into itself in ribbons without breaking or dropping off the spatula (like thick lava or honey). You can check the mixture is ready by holding the spatula above the bowl and slowly drawing a figure of 8 into the mixture; if the ribbon breaks, fold a few more times.

10 Load the mixture into a piping bag fitted with a medium open round nozzle.

11 Put the macaron mat on a baking tray and use the guides to pipe each shell by holding the piping bag vertically over the centre of each circle and squeezing gently. When the mixture reaches the inner circle, slightly swirl the tip around the macaron and pull away when the mix is halfway in-between the two lines. The mix shouldn't spread much, or just to the outer line on the macaron mat, but it should melt back into itself. Bang the tray on the surface several times to get rid of any air bubbles in the mix. Use a toothpick to pop any stubborn bubbles. The mixture should remain in a slight dome shape – if the macarons are flat, the mixture is too runny and you will have to start again.

12 Leave to rest for 30–60 minutes until the macaron shells develop a skin over the top.

13 Preheat the oven to 165°C (145°C fan/330°F/Gas 3). Every oven is different; it may take a few attempts to get to know your oven.

14 Put one baking tray in the oven at a time for 15–17 minutes. The macarons should rise with the signature feet and shiny tops. They should have a hard shell and not wobble when touched. If the feet wobble, put back into the oven for another minute and repeat until they do not move.

15 Remove from the oven and leave to cool completely on the baking tray. The macarons should easily lift off the mat. The shells can be frozen for up to 1 month. They can be kept at room temperature for up to a week.

BATTENBERG MACARONS

Pink and yellow macaron shells are sandwiched around marzipan, apricot jam and almond buttercream. This is a twist on the classic English cake with a surprise centre.

INGREDIENTS

Makes 20

150g (1¼ cups) icing sugar

140g (1⅓ cups) almond flour

90g (⅓ cup plus 1 tbsp) egg whites, at room temperature

¼ tsp cream of tartar

Pinch of salt

80g (6½ tbsp) caster sugar

2 tsp almond extract

Pink and yellow gel or powdered food colouring

Flavoured buttercream

100g (6½ tbsp) unsalted butter

200g (1⅔ cups) icing sugar

1 tsp almond extract, or to taste

Pink gel food colouring

Yellow gel food colouring

Filling

20g (¾oz) marzipan

2 tbsp smooth apricot jam

Decoration

Sprinkles (optional)

Flaked almonds (optional)

SPECIAL EQUIPMENT

Mixer or hand-held electric whisk

Piping bags, 2 Stuart #R18L nozzles (or any open round nozzle) and an Erin #1M nozzle (or nozzle of choice)

Macaron mat (see page 10)

5cm (2in) round pastry cutter

1 Follow steps 1–5 of the **BASIC MACARON SHELLS** recipe on page 216 using the quantities listed here, adding the almond extract. Do not add the colouring yet.

2 Add one-third of the almond flour and icing sugar mixture to the meringue and gently fold, using a figure of 8 action. This starts to knock the air out of the mixture. Add another third. Repeat.

3 Add the final third and fold again. The mixture may look and feel very thick and dry but will soon loosen. When just combined, put half of the mixture into another clean metal bowl. Add the pink gel colouring to one bowl and the yellow to the other. (Do not mix completely before adding the colours, as you will have to fold a few times to combine the colours, and overmixing will deflate the mix.) Continue to fold both until the consistency flows off your spatula like lava. Load each colour into a separate piping bag fitted with a medium open round nozzle.

4 Follow steps 11–15 of the **BASIC MACARON SHELLS** recipe (see page 219). Make the **FLAVOURED BUTTERCREAM**, using the quantities listed here (see page 16 for method) and flavour with the almond extract. Divide the buttercream between two bowls. Colour one portion pink and the other portion yellow. Load them into a piping bag fitted with your nozzle of choice, following the multi-tone piping technique (see page 24).

5 Roll out a thin layer of marzipan onto a work surface and cut out circles using a 5cm (2in) cutter. Alternatively, roll a small ball of marzipan in your hands and squash to the size of a macaron.

6 Pair up equal-sized macaron shells of the opposite colour. Put the apricot jam in a piping bag and snip off the end. Pipe a small blob of jam on one shell and stick a circle of marzipan down. Pipe a small circle of apricot jam on the marzipan.

7 Next, pipe a small circle of buttercream around the blob of apricot jam on the inner two-thirds of the macaron and press together with another shell. Repeat with the remaining shells. Leave plain or decorate with sprinkles and flaked almonds.

CANDY FLOSS MACARONS

The taste of candy floss, or cotton candy as it is known in the US, evokes childhood memories of sweet treats in fairgrounds, and these multicoloured macarons will leave a sweet taste in anyone's mouth – children and adults alike.

INGREDIENTS

Makes 20

150g (1¼ cups) icing sugar

140g (1⅓ cups) almond flour

90g (⅓ cup plus 1 tbsp) egg whites, at room temperature

¼ tsp cream of tartar

Pinch of salt

80g (6½ tbsp) caster sugar

1 tsp vanilla extract

Pink and blue gel or powdered food colouring

Flavoured buttercream

100g (6½ tbsp) unsalted butter

200g (1⅔ cups) icing sugar

¼ tsp candy floss extract, or to taste

Decoration

Sprinkles

SPECIAL EQUIPMENT

Mixer or hand-held electric whisk

Macaron mat (see page 00)

Piping bags and Stuart #R18L nozzle (or any open round nozzle) and Erin #1M nozzle (or nozzle of choice)

1 Follow steps 1–5 of the **BASIC MACARON SHELLS** recipe on page 216 using the quantities listed here, adding the vanilla extract. Do not add the colouring yet.

2 Add one-third of the almond flour and icing sugar mixture to the meringue and gently fold, using a figure of 8 action. This starts to knock the air out of the mixture.

3 When combined, add another third. Repeat the folding process.

4 Add the final third and fold again. The mixture may look and feel very thick and dry but will soon loosen. When just combined, put half of the mixture into another clean metal bowl. Add the pink gel to one bowl and the blue gel to the other. (Do not mix completely before adding the colours, as you will have to fold a few times to combine the colours, and overmixing will deflate the mix.) Continue to fold both until the consistency flows off your spatula like lava.

5 Using two tablespoons, drop alternating spoonfuls of each colour mixture into a piping bag fitted with an open round nozzle.

6 Follow steps 11–15 of the **BASIC MACARON SHELLS** recipe (see page 219).

7 Make the **FLAVOURED BUTTERCREAM** (see page 16) using the quantities listed here, adding the candy floss extract to taste.

8 Fill a piping bag fitted with your nozzle of choice with the buttercream. Pipe a small circle of buttercream in the inner two-thirds of a macaron shell and press together with another shell. Repeat with the remaining shells and buttercream.

9 Using colourful sprinkles, decorate the exposed edges of the buttercream before it sets.

CARAMEL MOCHA MACARONS

Whether it's a latte, cappuccino or flat white you prefer, these caramel, chocolate and whipped cream-filled coffee macarons will definitely hit the spot... with or without your afternoon cup!

INGREDIENTS

Makes 20

150g (1¼ cups) icing sugar

140g (1⅓ cups) almond flour

1 tbsp fine instant coffee

90g (⅓ cup plus 1 tbsp) egg whites, at room temperature

80g (6½ tbsp) caster sugar

¼ tsp cream of tartar

Pinch of salt

Ivory and dark brown gel or powdered food colouring

Milk chocolate ganache

200g (7oz) milk chocolate

100ml (6½ tbsp) double cream

Filling

2 tbsp caramel (see page 20 or use store-bought caramel sauce)

Whipped cream buttercream

85g (5½ tbsp) unsalted butter

165g (1⅓ cups) icing sugar

35ml (2½ tbsp) double cream

85g (3oz) white chocolate

Decoration

Cocoa powder, for dusting

Gold sprinkles (optional)

SPECIAL EQUIPMENT

Mixer or hand-held electric whisk

Piping bags and Stuart #R18L nozzle (or any open round nozzle) and Erin #1M nozzle (or nozzle of choice)

Paintbrush

Macaron mat (see page 10)

1 Before you start the macarons, make the ganache. Melt the milk chocolate with the double cream. Stir together and leave to set.

2 Follow steps 1–9 of the **BASIC MACARON SHELLS** recipe on pages 216 and 219 using the quantities listed here, adding the coffee to the food processor in step 1 and colouring the mix with the ivory gel food colouring in step 6 to achieve a light caramel colour.

3 Place a medium open round nozzle in the end of a piping bag, take a paintbrush loaded with dark brown gel colouring and paint a few lines up and all around the inside of the bag – this will create a two-tone colour effect on top of your macarons. Continue with steps 10–15 of the **BASIC MACARON SHELLS** recipe (see page 219).

4 Once cool, pair up the macarons into matching halves. Fill a piping bag with the caramel sauce, snip off the end and pipe a small circle into the centre of one shell.

5 If the milk chocolate ganache has hardened, heat it in the microwave at full power in 5-second bursts until loosened. Load it into a piping bag, snip off the end and pipe a small circle of milk chocolate ganache around the blob of caramel sauce on the inner two-thirds of the macaron. Reserve a little ganache for decorating.

6 Prepare a small batch of **WHIPPED CREAM BUTTERCREAM** (see page 17) using the quantities listed here. On the other shell half, pipe a ring of whipped cream buttercream using a piping bag fitted with your nozzle of choice. Press the pair of shells together. Repeat with the remaining shells.

7 Dust with cocoa powder and drizzle with the reserved melted ganache. Add gold sprinkles, if you like.

TOP TIP ★ You could use a small amount of the dark brown gel if you don't have ivory colouring.

UNICORN MACARONS

These cute unicorn-shaped macarons are filled with candy floss buttercream, sprinkles and glitter, and will bring a little bit of magic to any celebration.

INGREDIENTS

Makes 20

200g (1¾ cups) icing sugar

185g (1½ cups) almond flour

120g (½ cup) egg whites, at room temperature

½ tsp cream of tartar

Pinch of salt

110g (½ cup) caster sugar

Pink gel or powdered food colouring

Vanilla extract, to taste

Flavoured buttercream

100g (6½ tbsp) unsalted butter

200g (1¾ cups) icing sugar

1 tsp candy floss extract (optional)

Pink gel food colouring

Purple gel food colouring

Blue gel food colouring

Decoration

Sprinkles

Gold lustre dust (plus lemon juice, vodka or gin), for the horn

Black edible food art pen or black gel food colouring, pink edible food art pen and edible glitter

SPECIAL EQUIPMENT

Mixer or hand-held electric whisk

Macaron mat (see page 10)

Piping bags, Stuart #R18L nozzle (or open round nozzle) and Mandy #R3 nozzle and Erin #1M nozzle (or nozzles of choice)

Paintbrush

Printed unicorn macaron template (optional)

1 Follow steps 1–10 of the **BASIC MACARON SHELLS** recipe on pages 216 and 219, using the quantities listed here and adding a touch of pink gel food colouring and vanilla extract to the mix in step 6.

2 Continue with step 11 and use a small writing nozzle to free-hand the horn and ears. Alternatively, you can use a scriber tool to pull the mixture into place, and there also are unicorn-shaped macaron mats available to purchase.

3 Continue with steps 12–15 of the **BASIC MACARON SHELLS** (see page 219).

4 Once cooled, match up the macaron shells to size. Prepare a batch of **FLAVOURED BUTTERCREAM** (see page 16) using the quantities listed here and add the candy floss extract (or more to taste), if using. Use the multi-tone piping technique (see page 24), using pink, purple and blue gel food colouring to load a piping bag fitted with your nozzle of choice. Pipe a circle in the inner two-thirds of one macaron shell. Press together with another shell. Repeat with the rest.

5 Decorate the exposed edges of buttercream with sprinkles before it sets.

6 Mix a shaking of gold lustre dust with a couple of drops of lemon juice or spirit – vodka or gin works best. Use a paintbrush to mix together and gently paint onto the horn and ears. Leave to dry.

7 Using the remaining buttercream, pipe three tiny rosettes onto each shell to mimic a mane. Use a black edible food art pen or a small paintbrush with black gel food colouring to draw on the eyes, lashes and nose. Use a pink edible food art pen to draw the pink ears and cheeks.

8 Finish with adding more sprinkles to the mane and some edible glitter.

STRAWBERRY DOUGHNUT MACARONS

What's more fun than food shaped like other food?! This is a strawberry buttercream-filled "doughnut" with rainbow sprinkles... but in macaron form! There's nothing not to love.

INGREDIENTS

Makes 15

150g (1¼ cups) icing sugar

140g (1⅓ cups) almond flour

90g (⅓ cup plus 1 tbsp) egg whites, at room temperature

¼ tsp cream of tartar

Pinch of salt

80g (6½ tbsp) caster sugar

Pink gel or powdered food colouring

1 tsp vanilla extract

Flavoured buttercream

100g (6½ tbsp) unsalted butter

200g (1⅔ cups) icing sugar

4 drops of strawberry flavouring, or to taste

Decoration

200g (1⅔ cups) icing sugar

Pink gel food colouring

Sprinkles and edible glitter

SPECIAL EQUIPMENT

Mixer or hand-held electric whisk

Piping bags and Stuart #R18L nozzle (or open round nozzle) and Erin #1M nozzle (or nozzle of choice)

Macaron mat (see page 10, optional)

1 Follow steps 1–9 of the **BASIC MACARON SHELLS** recipe on pages 216 and 219 using the quantities listed here, remembering to add a touch of pink gel food colouring and vanilla extract in step 6.

2 Load the mixture into a piping bag fitted with a medium round nozzle. Line a baking tray with parchment or a macaron mat. Pipe macaron-sized circles with even pressure, swirling the nozzle around the "doughnut" and gently lifting off. You can draw your own guide to ensure the circles are all the same size, or, if using a macaron mat with a double halo, use the centre ring as a guide. Bang the tray on the work surface to get rid of any air bubbles. Use a toothpick to pop any stubborn bubbles.

3 Leave to rest for 30–60 minutes until the shells develop a skin over the top. Preheat the oven to 160°C (140°C fan/325°F/Gas 3).

4 Bake one tray at a time for 13 minutes. The macarons should rise with signature feet and shiny tops. They should have a hard shell and not wobble when touched. If the feet wobble, put back into the oven for another minute until they do not move.

5 Leave to cool completely on the baking tray. The macarons should easily lift off the baking tray.

6 Match up the shells into pairs of even shape. Prepare a batch of **FLAVOURED BUTTERCREAM** (see page 16) using the quantities listed here, and adding the strawberry flavouring. Using your nozzle of choice, pipe blobs around the flat side of one shell and press together with the matching shell.

7 For the decoration, make a small batch of glacé icing by adding a few drops of water to the icing sugar and stirring to a thickened consistency. Colour it pink. Load into a piping bag, snip the very end off and carefully draw a circle around the centre hole and then another wavy line around the outside.

8 Add sprinkles and edible glitter, and leave the icing to set.

ICE CREAM CONE CUPCAKES

This recipe is so versatile, you can change the cake flavour, fillings and colours of these ice cream cone cupcakes to suit any occasion!

INGREDIENTS

Makes 12

12 flat-bottomed ice cream cones

180g (1½ sticks) unsalted butter or baking margarine

180g (¾ cup plus 2 tbsp) caster sugar

3 eggs

180g (1⅔ cups) self-raising flour

2 tsp vanilla extract (optional)

12 tsp jam of choice

Vanilla buttercream

250g (2 sticks) unsalted butter

500g (3½ cups) icing sugar, sifted

2 tsp vanilla extract

Decoration

Sprinkles, dessert sauce and chocolate flakes

SPECIAL EQUIPMENT

Baking sheet, lined

Mixer or hand-held electric whisk

Piping bag and Isabel #9FE or Emily #1E nozzle (or nozzle of choice)

1   Preheat the oven to 180°C (160°C fan/350°F/Gas 4).

2   Lay out 12 flat-bottomed ice cream cones on a lined baking sheet.

3   Using a mixer with the paddle attachment (or a hand-held electric whisk), beat the softened butter and caster sugar together until creamed. When combined, scrape down the sides of the bowl with a spatula and repeat. On a medium speed, slowly add the eggs, one by one. Sift in the self-raising flour and mix until just combined, along with the vanilla extract, if using. Do not overmix! Remember to scrape down the sides and bottom of the bowl.

4   Scoop up some of the batter with one teaspoon and gently scrape it off with a second teaspoon into the bottom of each ice cream cone. Fill each cone around two-thirds full, weighing each to create an even batch.

5   Bake in the preheated oven for 20–23 minutes, or until a toothpick, inserted into the middle of the sponge, comes out clean.

6   Take the cones out of the oven and leave to cool on the baking sheet (being careful not to knock them over). When completely cool, use a teaspoon to cut around the border where the cake and cone meet, creating a removable lid. Spoon a teaspoon of jam into the hole and replace the lid.

7   Make the **VANILLA BUTTERCREAM** following the recipe on page 16, using the quantities listed here. Load it into a piping bag with your nozzle of choice. Twist the piping bag at the top and hold one hand over this twist and the other to guide. With an even pressure, pipe from the outside of the cone inwards to create a peak or a "whip". Repeat for each one.

8   Decorate using sprinkles, dessert sauce and chocolate flakes.

TERMS & TRANSLATIONS

British ingredients	American ingredients
bicarbonate of soda	baking soda
Biscoff biscuits	Belgian wafer cookies
Biscoff spread	creamy cookie butter, Trader Joe's Speculoos Butter is an ideal substitute
biscuits	cookies
black treacle	molasses
candy floss	cotton candy
caster sugar	superfine sugar
chocolate spread	Trader Joe's has a chocolate/almond spread, US bakers can find Cadbury chocolate spread online at Amazon
cornflour	cornstarch
digestive biscuits	Graham crackers
double cream	heavy cream
flaked almonds	sliced almonds
ginger biscuits	ginger thins cookies, such as Anna's or Peek Freans Ginger Crisps
golden syrup	Light corn syrup is a barely adequate substitute. Whole Foods usually stocks authentic golden syrup.
icing sugar	confectioners' sugar
Jammie Dodgers	jelly ring cookies
Lotus biscuits	see Biscoff biscuits
Lotus spread	see Biscoff spread
mixed spice	apple pie spice
plain flour	all-purpose flour
self-raising flour	self-rising flour
soured cream	sour cream
sponge	cake
sultanas	golden raisins

British equipment	American equipment
cake drum	cake board
cake scraper	cake icing smoother or comb (available at Wilton's)
cake tin	cake pan
cling film	plastic wrap
cocktail stick	toothpick
hob	stovetop burner
nozzle	piping tip
piping bag	pastry bag
sugar thermometer	candy thermometer

CONVERSIONS

If required, we recommend you follow the conversions as listed on the individual recipes, however, here is a handy list of standard conversions should you need them for anything else.

Dry measures

15g	½oz
30g	1oz
60g	2oz
90g	3oz
125g	4oz (¼lb)
155g	5oz
185g	6oz
220g	7oz
250g	8oz (½lb)
280g	9oz
315g	10oz
345g	11oz
375g	12oz (¾lb)
410g	13oz
440g	14oz
470g	15oz
500g	16oz (1lb)
750g	24oz (1½lb)
1kg	32oz (2lb)

Volume measures

75ml	2½fl oz
90ml	3fl oz
100ml	3½fl oz
120ml	4fl oz
150ml	5fl oz
200ml	7fl oz
240ml	8fl oz
250ml	9fl oz
300ml	10fl oz
350ml	12fl oz
400ml	14fl oz
450ml	15fl oz
500ml	16fl oz
600ml	1 pint
750ml	1¼ pints
900ml	1½ pints
1 litre	1¾ pints
1.2 litres	2 pints
1.4 litres	2½ pints
1.5 litres	2¾ pints
1.7 litres	3 pints
2 litres	3½ pints
3 litres	5¼ pints

Length measures

3mm	⅛in
6mm	¼in
1cm	½in
2cm	¾in
2.5cm	1in
5cm	2in
6cm	2½in
8cm	3in
10cm	4in
13cm	5in
15cm	6in
18cm	7in
20cm	8in
22cm	9in
25cm	10in
28cm	11in
30cm	12in (1ft)

Oven temperatures

130°C	110°C fan/250°F/Gas ½
140°C	120°C fan/275°F/Gas 1
150°C	130°C fan/300°F/Gas 2
160°C	140°C fan/325°F/Gas 3
180°C	160°C fan/350°F/Gas 4
190°C	170°C fan/375°F/Gas 5
200°C	180°C fan/400°F/Gas 6
220°C	200°C fan/425°F/Gas 7
230°C	210°C fan/455°F/Gas 8
240°C	220°C fan/475°F/Gas 9

Australian tablespoon conversions to UK spoon measures

½ tbsp	2 tsp
1 tbsp	1 heaped tbsp
2 tbsp (8 tsp)	2½ tbsp
3 tbsp (12 tsp)	4 tbsp
4 tbsp (16 tsp)	5 tbsp
5 tbsp (20 tsp)	6½ tbsp
6 tbsp (24 tsp)	8 tbsp

INDEX

ACKNOWLEDGEMENTS

Thank you to Steph, Bess, Kiron, Kate and everybody at DK for seeing our passion and working alongside us to help develop our ideas. Dominique and Jess, thank you for styling, pipetting, tweezing and shooting to make this the beautifully photographed book you see today. To Jack, our friend, website designer and now book designer, thanks so much for chatting to us all hours about anything and everything, and making our vision come to life.

To our Mum, Dad and brother: Leanne, Stuart and Thomas – we will forever be in debt to the hard work and passion you all have for Finch Bakery and for running sides of our business that we wouldn't have a clue about.

To Dec and Ed, thank you for being there from day one, from bringing us coffee and energy drinks when we worked 18-hour days at the shop to helping serve on a Saturday morning, as well as now being amazing daddies to our gorgeous children. We love you (most of the time).

To every colleague, past, present and future, who has worked so hard for us and helped us build such a dream business. We are so happy and proud to call you our baking family and we are so excited to see where Finch Bakery is going next with you all. Special mention to our OG's, Tessa, Isabel, Hannah, Gillian and our Mum for the all-nighters, witnessing stress-induced farguments (Finch arguments) and Nutella/ baking tray incidents...

To the baking community all over the UK; thank you for the long chats, rants, questions, advice and genuine friendships both online and in real life. To all the people, accounts, professionals and home bakers from whom we get inspiration, and who are, in turn, inspired by us.

To our best friends; Evie, Jade, Katie, Smella, Claire, Holly, Baines, Joe, Tessa and Leanne. Thank you for supporting our business, helping out for free cake in the early days, trying out all our recipes and listening to our dramas over the past year and beyond. We couldn't do life without you, huns. x

Finally, the biggest thank you is to our customers. Whether you have followed us from our home kitchen days, visited the shop once or twice, ordered every week, watched from afar or are reading about us for the first time today, we would be nowhere without you all. Thank you to each and every one of you for supporting us, buying from us, following our lives and now, recreating our recipes.

Lauren & Rachel x

To see all the treats, equipment and baking ingredients that Finch Bakery have to offer, visit **www.finchbakery.com**

Publishing Director Katie Cowan
Art Director Maxine Pedliham
Senior Acquisitions Editor Stephanie Milner
Managing Art Editor Bess Daly
Editor Kiron Gill
Copy Editor Kate Reeves-Brown
US Editor Susan Stuck
Designer Jack Watkins
Proofreader Anne Sheasby
Indexer Hilary Bird
Jackets Coordinator Lucy Philpott
Production Editor Heather Blagden
Production Controller Stephanie McConnell
Creative Technical Support Sonia Charbonnier
Prop Stylist Charlie Phillips
Food Stylist Dominique Eloïse Alexander
Photography by Jessica Griffiths

First published in Great Britain in 2021 by
Dorling Kindersley Limited
DK, One Embassy Gardens, 8 Viaduct Gardens,
London, SW11 7BW

The authorised representative in the EEA is
Dorling Kindersley Verlag GmbH.
Arnulfstr. 124, 80636 Munich, Germany

A CIP catalogue record for this book
is available from the British Library.
ISBN: 978-0-2415-1510-5

Printed and bound in the UK

For the curious

www.dk.com

This book was made with Forest Stewardship
Council ™ certified paper – one small step
in DK's commitment to a sustainable future.

For more information go to
www.dk.com/our-green-pledge